STUDY GUIDE on Shakespeare's

OTHELLO

MADE SUPER SUPER EASY

TEXT EXPLAINED IN GREAT DETAIL

ACHIEVE TOP GRADES
A MUST FOR ALL STUDENTS

EVELYN SAMUEL on Shakespeare

Shakespeare's Othello
Made Super Super Easy
First Edition Published by Evelyn Samuel

EveMadeSuperEasyBooks
www.EveSuperEasyBooks.com
evesupereasybooks@gmail.com

DEDICATED TO

Dr Kelvin P
A Man's A Man for A' That
Balliol College Oxford

There is a star whose beaming ray
Is shed on ev'ry clime.
It shines by night, it shines by day
And ne'er grows dim wi' time.

Away, ye gay landscapes, ye gardens of roses !
In you let the minions of luxury rove,
Restore me the rocks where the snow-flake reposes,
If still they are sacred to freedom and love.

Tis there for honest poverty.

REVIEWS

☆☆☆☆☆ **Othello dissected**

Reviewed 05 May 2021

Dissects in detail all facets that makes Shakespeare's Othello such a compelling antagonistic love story.

☆☆☆☆☆ **A great study guide!**

Reviewed 26 November 2021

I needed a concise understanding of the characters, the plot, and interactions to help me achieve the best grade possible. I found it in this study guide made super super easy.

PREFACE

To all students reading my study guide **Othello made super super easy**. I do hope that my wealth of information will assist you to achieve the highest possible grades. I have formulated a unique structure where detailed explanations are next to the text to make it super super easy for you to connect and understand the book, and to revise without the need to resort to more than one book.

Each scene is defined by a Summary followed by in-depth explanations to the text which is highlighted with relevant important quotes. It identifies connotated meaning, imagery, symbolism, and linguistic devices. The context identifies the rationale behind the book, so that although Shakespeare wrote the play as a jealous-hate tragedy, the play essentially revolves around the historical events happening in the Mediterranean where the Venetians are battling against the Ottoman Turk for control of Cyprus.

Character descriptions and themes are included to provide perspective in understanding the storyline. Typical exam questions are included to give some idea of the scope sought by the Exam Boards. Further details can be found in the Specification published by the Exam Boards on their websites.

Good Luck with your studies and your exam results.

FOREWARD

What a **super super easy** way to study and understand Shakespeare's 'Othello'. No need to match text with explanation when both are next to each other.

I really enjoyed looking left at the text and right at the explanation. The structure and content of this fantastic Study Guide is a solid base to get to grip with the intricacies of Shakespeare's black and white plot of jealousy by Othello, and hatred by Iago, the nemesis of Othello.

I can without reservation recommend this study guide to all students, and hope they gain as much insight, as I did, into Shakespeare's 'Othello'.

Teacher of English

BOOKS PUBLISHED IN THE SERIES
MADE SUPER SUPER EASY

Shakespeare's
MACBETH
ROMEO AND JULIET

Priestley's
AN INSPECTOR CALLS

Dickens'
A CHRISTMAS CAROL

SOON TO FOLLOW IN THE SERIES
MADE SUPER SUPER EASY

Shakespeare's
THE TEMPEST
TWELFTH NIGHT
A MIDSUMMER NIGHT'S DREAM
THE MERCHANT OF VENICE

www.EveSuperEasyBooks.com
EveSuperEasyBooks@gmail.com

CONTENTS

INTRODUCTION		**11**
SHAKESPEARE		11
PLAY		11
CONTEXT		11
THE PLAY		**13**
CHARACTERS		13
SYNOPSIS		14
SETTING		16
FORM		16
STRUCTURE		17
LANGUAGE		17
TEXT AND EXPLANATIONS		**22**
ACT 1		
Summary		23
Scene 1	Roderigo upset with Iago for not promoting marriage to Desdemona	24
Scene 2	Brabantio accuses Othello of bewitching his daughter Desdemona	30
Scene 3	Iago will help Roderigo seduce Desdemona to discredit Othello	34
ACT 2		
Summary		46
Scene 1	Iago persuades Roderigo to provoke and discredit Cassio	47
Scene 2	Peace in Cyprus and belated celebration of Othello's marriage	57
Scene 3	Roderigo fights Cassio, Othello sacks Cassio, Iago manipulates both	58
ACT 3		
Summary		70
Scene 1	Iago wife Emilia agrees to get Cassio reinstated via Desdemona	71
Scene 2	Othello and nemesis Iago set out to inspect town fortifications	74
Scene 3	Othello promotes Iago and asks him to kill Cassio	75
Scene 4	Desdemona pleads for Cassio, but Othello believes they are lovers	91
ACT 4		
Summary		99
Scene 1	Othello vows to murder Desdemona over suspected adultery	100
Scene 2	Othello confronts Desdemona, trying to get her to confess	111
Scene 3	Desdemona and Emilia discuss female infidelity	120
ACT 5		
Summary		124
Scene 1	Cassio wounds Roderigo, Iago stabs Cassio then kills Roderigo	125
Scene 2	Othello kills Desdemona, Iago's plot is revealed, Othello kills himself	131

CHARACTERS **145**

OTHELLO 145
DESDEMONA 146
IAGO 147
RODERIGO 148
EMILIA 149
CASSIO 150

THEMES **151**

JEALOUSY 151
RACISM 152
LOVE, RELATIONSHIP, FRIENDSHIP 153

EXAM STYLE QUESTIONS **154**

AUTHOR **157**

INTRODUCTION

SHAKESPEARE

Famous as an Elizabethan playwright, Shakespeare captivated his audience with his imaginative scenes and dialogue. Most of his plays are based on imaginative and real events elsewhere in the world. Although not much is known about his day-to-day life, the wealth of information built into his plays, indicates he had an extensive knowledge of world places and customs, but more importantly, an understanding of the human physique: what made the audience weep, laugh, rage, enjoy and identify with the play.

PLAY

Shakespeare wrote Othello in circa 1603, melding historical events such as the Ottoman-Venetian War circa 1570 with the human physique of jealousy and lust. The renowned Moorish general Othello hired by the Venetian, is manipulated by his nemesis Iago into a state of jealousy, resulting in Othello's killing his wife Desdemona and later himself on realization of his gross folly.

CONTEXT

- Othello was written during the Elizabethan era. It is an Elizabethan/Jacobean revenge tragedy with a psychologically driven plot and a dire quest for revenge by the antagonist, Iago.
- Many of the Machiavellian elements ingrained in Othello can be seen in Greek Tragedies where we see the downfall of the hero who becomes a tragic hero and Othello fits perfectly into this category. We see his rise and fall through his hamartia – his unwavering trust in Iago, his hubris – his inability to discover the truth and peripeteia – finding out about the handkerchief and the catharsis - the overwhelming sense of horror that instilled both fear and pity in the audience who, in the end feel relieved from their repressed emotions because everyone paid adequately for their misdeeds.
- The Renaissance period saw a revival of artistic and cultural development through poetry and literature.
- The play is set in Venice in the 16th Century at the time when the country was engaged in a war with the Ottoman Empire.
- It was uncommon in Elizabethan society to have Moorish Othello play a significant role in Venetian society.
- Black people were treated differently as seen in Brabantio's, Iago's and Emilia's derogatory treatment of Othello.

- In the Elizabethan and Jacobean era, women assumed subordinate, inferior roles to men but Shakespeare created strong female characters who broke social norms and paid the ultimate price for it. Women were subservient to men as seen in Desdemona's loyalty to Othello and her life was controlled by patriarchy.
- Fathers were expected to choose spouses for their daughters hence Brabantio's fury when Desdemona made her own choice. Brabantio viewed Desdemona as his 'property.'
- Assertive and strong-willed women like Emilia were publicly shamed or punished by the 'ducking' stool.
- Even women's intellectual ability and thought processes were undermined and were thought to be inferior to that of men.
- The underlying theme in Othello is sexual jealousy, Venice was associated with villainy and decadence, hence Shakespeare spiced this Jacobean play with Bianca as a sexually jealous courtesan who is a public mockery and an outcast as seen by her shabby treatment by Iago, Emilia and even Cassio.
- Iago classed Desdemona as a decent, classy, sexually sophisticated woman from Venetian high society.
- This can be true because Desdemona couldn't believe that women can be unfaithful to their husbands and vowed that she will never do such a degrading thing.
- During the Renaissance period, many dramas contained Machiavellian characters who were evil and downright destructive as seen in Iago's malevolent and cynical exploitation of the characters to achieve his own desires.
- In the end these antagonists ultimately get the punishment they rightfully deserve.

CHARACTERS

A list of the CHARACTERS and their RELATIONSHIPS

CHARACTER																RELATIONSHIP
ACT	1			2			3				4			5		ACT
SCENE	1	2	3	1	2	3	1	2	3	4	1	2	3	1	2	SCENE
FAMILY																FAMILY
Othello																The Moor
Desdemona																Othello's wife
Brabantio																wife's father
Clown																servant
Herald																Othello's
ANTAGONISTS																ANTAGONISTS
Iago																Ensign
Emilia																Iago's wife
Cassio																lieutenant
Roderigo																Venetian
VENETIANS																VENETIANS
Lodovico																Brabantio man
Gratiano																Brabantio man
Duke																
Senator 1																
Senator 2																
Officer																
Sailor																
Musician																
CYPRIANS																CYPRIANS
Montano																Ex-governor
Bianca																Cassio's lover
Messenger																
Gentleman 1																
Gentleman 2																
Gentleman 3																
SCENE	1	2	3	1	2	3	1	2	3	4	1	2	3	1	2	SCENE
ACT	1			2			3				4			5		ACT
CHARACTER																RELATIONSHIP

SYNOPSIS

In Act I, love is the theme. The Moorish general Othello has secretly married Desdemona, the daughter of a wealthy Venetian family. Roderigo a jealous suitor of Desdemona, informs her father Brabantio who immediately goes in search of Othello and accuses him of bewitching his daughter. The Duke of Venice intercedes but Brabantio disowns his daughter even though Desdemona and Othello declare their love for each other. The senate decide that Othello should be the general to defend Cyprus from the forthcoming Turkish invasion. Desdemona asks to be allowed to accompany her husband, which is granted but she is put in the care of Emilia, Iago's wife, as lady-in-waiting. Iago is Othello's ensign who has served with him on previous military campaigns, but is a self-seeking opportunistic, who becomes Othello's nemesis. Brabantio warns Othello against trusting Desdemona, and Iago schemes to help Roderigo seduce Desdemona.

In Act 2, conflict is the theme. The Turkish fleet is destroyed by a storm, but Othello and his entourage arrive safely in Cyprus. Iago dislikes Cassio, Othello's lieutenant, and makes Roderigo believe that Cassio is his rival for Desdemona's affections. On the night of victory celebrations, Iago gets Cassio drunk, and undermines Cassio's reputation by informing Montano, the previous governor of Cyprus, that Cassio is a drunkard. Iago then goads Roderigo into picking a fight with Cassio, in which Montano is accidentally wounded. The fight is stopped by Othello on his arrival, with the consequence that Cassio is dismissed from his military post and disgraced. Iago, who has planned all, persuades Cassio to let Desdemona plead his case for reinstatement. To action this plan, Iago persuades Emilia, his wife, to promote Cassio's cause with Desdemona while poisoning Othello's mind with the idea that Cassio and Desdemona are lovers.

In Act 3, jealousy is the theme. Cassio hires musicians to serenade Othello and Desdemona, but in response, Othello sends his clown to tell them to go. While Othello and Iago are away inspecting the fortifications, Cassio and Emilia persuade Desdemona to plead Cassio's cause, but when Othello returns, he spots Cassio leaving, and is suspicious of his wife's motives in supporting Cassio's cause. This is further fuelled when later Iago hints that Desdemona has committed adultery with Cassio. Jealousy begins to take hold. Meanwhile, Desdemona drops her handkerchief which is picked up by Emilia and later given to Iago. Iago see an opportunity to use the handkerchief as a weapon to support the adultery claim and tells Othello that Cassio had called out for Desdemona in a dream and had been seen wiping his beard with the handkerchief that Othello had given Desdemona as a token of their love.

Othello enraged, tells Iago that in three days he expects him to say that Cassio is not alive. With that, Othello promotes Iago to lieutenant. Desdemona asks the clown to inform Cassio that she is still pleading his case. Othello challenges Desdemona about the lost handkerchief, but she cannot produce it which annoys Othello. He is becoming convinced that what Iago has said is true. Meanwhile, Cassio's mistress Bianca, is also annoyed because Cassio has neglected her. Cassio gives her the handkerchief, saying he found it in his bed chamber.

In Act 4, torment is the theme. Iago torments Othello with crude images of Desdemona's infidelity and persuades Othello to observe him talking to Cassio. Not being able to hear, but seeing Desdemona's handkerchief in Bianca's hand, and believing that Desdemona must have given it to Cassio as a love token, Othello vows to murder Desdemona. Rather than poisoning her, Iago suggests smothering her in the martial bed. Bianca returns the handkerchief to Cassio. Next, Lodovico arrives with news that Othello is to return to Venice and Cassio is to take his place. Desdemona also arrives, but Othello is seething, and ends up striking Desdemona. Lodovico is shocked. Later, Othello questions Emilia but is not convinced that she is telling the truth about Desdemona's actions. Then, Othello confronts Desdemona, to see if she will confess to adultery, but she remains firm, declaring her innocence. Not being able to get Emilia to condemn Desdemona, Othello gives her money to keep quiet about recent events. Desdemona appeals to Iago for help, but Iago, the instigator of Desdemona's woes, is duplicitous, and assures her it is a misunderstanding, too much pressure of state on Othello. Scheming as ever, Iago persuades Roderigo to kill Cassio. Othello with thoughts of murder, and Iago suggestion of smothering Desdemona in their bed, sends her to prepare for bed. Together, Desdemona and Emilia talk about female infidelity. Desdemona says she still loves Othello, and Emilia says she wishes Desdemona had never met him. Desdemona is unable to dismiss a melancholy song from her mind which she sings.

In Act 5, justice is the theme. Roderigo is wounded by Cassio, but Iago stabs Cassio in the leg who is then attended by Lodovico and Gratiano. To cover up the plot, Iago kills Roderigo, and then accuses Bianca of taking part in the plot to kill Cassio. Gripped by jealousy, Othello smothers Desdemona in their bed, still protesting her innocence. Emilia finds Desdemona on the verge of death, proclaiming that Othello is not to blame for her death. Emilia raises the alarm, Iago arrives, stabs Emilia in revenge for revealing his dastardly scheme to kill Othello and leaves her to die on the bed next to Desdemona. Guards return with Iago who is then wounded by Othello. Realising his folly, Othello kills himself and dies next to Desdemona. Iago is led away, and Cassio is made governor of Cyprus.

SETTING

The two principal locations are Venice in Italy and the island of Cyprus. The most poignant scenes are inside buildings, and in particular the matrimonial bedroom.

At the end of the sixteenth century, dramatists made use of Venice as a setting for tragedies because of its renaissance history encompassing elements of power, culture, wealth, and intrigue. In particular, the sophisticated culture mix generated by trade which led to people from many different countries to visit and live in the city. Othello the Moor being one of them.

Shakespeare uses the Ottoman invasion of Cyprus to create a platform where jealousy, hate, rivalry, ambition, violence, and lust lurk in a Machiavellian world of deceit and cunning, all too familiar to Italian cities like Venice. Iago being the principal Machiavellian architect in Othello's downfall.

FORM

Shakespeare's Othello takes the form of a play made up entirely of dialogue where the audience discover through words delivered by actors, the type of characters, their motives, their relationships together with the storyline.

Shakespeare's aim was to educate and entertain ordinary people in an age when few people could read - to draw out the emotions in people. In this case, to expose the dark side of human desire where jealousy, lust and ambition destroy love through connivance and deceit.

The dialogue is in three different forms: mainly blank verse, prose and rhyming verse. Each line of blank verse, is made up of roughly ten syllables, organised into five groups of two, where an unstressed syllable is followed by a stressed syllable. This creates an air of authority and identifies higher status characters such as Desdemona from lower characters such as servants who speak in ordinary prose.

Rhyming verse is used by Shakespeare to end lines in a memorable way so that the audience recall it in later scenes; to make characters complete each other's rhymes to emphasise unity in thought, action, ideas and moods between them.

STRUCTURE

The play *'Othello'* is edited into five Acts, each containing several scenes. The storyline is straightforward based on the classical five-part structure:

•an initial incident - termed **Exposition**
•a growth in tension - termed **Rising Action**
•a climax to the drama - termed **Climax**
•an unravelling of the plot - termed **Falling Action**
•a resolution to the drama - termed **Denouement**

There are no subplots and therefore the play conforms to the structure of place, action and time. The action moves apace from the opening fight scene to the closing tragic deaths of Desdemona by Othello and then himself by his own hand. The short time frame of a few days secures the interest of the audience as events move swift-on leaving no time for the audience to anticipate the next event.

The Soliloquy is a structure used by Shakespeare to present a deeper insight into the characters.

"And what's he then that says I play the villain ..." (spoken by Iago Act 2 scene 3)
"Her father loved me, oft invited me ..." (spoken by Othello Act 1 scene 3)
"It is the cause ..." (spoken by Othello Act 5 scene 2)
"Like to the Pontic ..." (spoken by Othello Act 3 scene 3)
"That I did love the Moor ..." (spoken by Desdemona Act 1 scene 3)
"Virtue! A fig! ..." (spoken by Iago Act 1 scene 3)

LANGUAGE

Shakespeare makes use of speech, imagery, and irony to create, enrich and maintain the Machiavellian plot where Iago is determined to manipulate others to achieve his goals: the destruction of Othello in favour of his own meteoric rise.

SPEECH

The language device of **speech** is used by Shakespeare to establish Othello's heroism, nobility, and authority, early on in the play.

"Keep up your bright swords ..." (spoken by Othello Act 1 scene 2)
"Most potent, grave, and reverend signiors ..." (spoken by Othello Act 1 scene 3)

Shakespeare makes most of Othello's long speeches poetic, expressing the nobility and romance of a true protagonist, but this changes as jealousy consumes verse, and replaces it by disjointed prose.

"Lie with her? Lie on her? We say ..." (spoken by Othello Act 4 scene 1)

Juxtaposed to Othello, Iago speech is full of colloquialisms and oaths, most powerfully expressed in his soliloquies early in the play. Finally, when confronted with his villainous deeds, Iago evokes power by his defiant silence.

"Demand me nothing ... I never will speak word." (spoken by Iago Act 5 scene 2)

It is ironic that Iago's wife Emilia is the one that shatters his power of words by exposing their villainous intent.

IMAGERY

Shakespeare uses **imagery** to reinforce the themes of jealousy, race and colour, heroism, and personal conflict.

Black and White is the imagery of darkness and light, hell and heaven, and are related to the central paradox in the play where Othello is the virtuous heavenly hero with a white soul, while Iago is the devilish fiend with a black soul. However, later in the play, Othello's heart is poisoned by Iago's black lies, and he calls for revenge.

"Arise, black vengeance, from thy hollow cell" (spoken by Othello Act 3 scene 3)

Throughout the play, Desdemona is associated with images of purity and light. Even Othello is not entirely convinced that she is guilty as he prepares to kill her.

"Put out the light, then put out the light" (spoken by Othello Act 5 scene 2)

It is interesting that most of the scenes occur at night. Othello's first entrance occurs at night, and the murder of Desdemona, also at night. Not only has he fulfilled his tragic destiny by putting out Desdemona's light but also his own. Iago is the darkness that Othello has embraced.

Animals and Insects is the imagery of base behaviour and self-interest.

"Plague him with flies" (spoken by Iago Act 1 scene 1)
"an old black ram is tupping your white ewe" (spoken by Iago Act 1 scene 1)
"led by th' nose as ass are" (spoken by Iago Act 1 scene 3)
"With as little a web as this will I ensnare as great a fly as Cassio" (spoken by Iago Act 2 scene 1)

In Act 3 scene 3, Othello expresses his misery, rather than triumph, in response to Iago's falsehoods about Cassio.

"I had rather be a toad
And live upon this vapour of a dungeon
Than keep a corner in a thing I love
For others' uses"

Later, in Act 3 scene 3, Iago stokes Othello's jealousy by referring to Cassio and Desdemona in bestial terms.

"Were they as as prime as goats, as hot as monkeys,
As salt as wolves in pride"

Othello is devoid of reason and accepts the sexual images espoused by Iago.

The last animal imagery in the play encapsulates the villain of the play when Lodovico addresses Iago by the title, "O Spartan dog", where Iago is a servant to evil as were the Spartan to their State, totally subservient.

Devil and Hell is the imagery of Iago and makes the link himself at the end of his soliloquy in Act 1 scene 3.

"Hell and night
Must bring this monstrous birth to the world's light"

Later in Act 2 scene 3, Iago in his soliloquy uses the **oxymoron**, "Divinity of hell", and explains to the audience,

"When devils will their blackest sins put on
They do suggest at first with heavenly shows
As I do now"

There are other references to the imagery of the **devil and hell**, which permeate the play to emphasis the darkness within the play

"Lest, being like one of heaven, the devils themselves" (spoken by Othello Act 4 scene 2)
"And keeps the gates of hell" (spoken by Othello Act 4 scene 2)
"And you the blacker devill" (spoken by Emilia Act 5 scene 2)

In the final scene of the play, Act 5 scene 2, Othello bewildered by Iago's evil machinations, says to Cassio,

"Will you, I pray, demand that demi-devil
Why he hath thus ensnared my soul and body?"

Poisoning is the imagery of malicious intent, generated in thought and put into deed. The main proponent is Iago who gradually infects Othello with the same intent.

In Act 1 scene 1, Iago says to Roderigo when speaking about Brabantio, Desdemona's father, that he wants to "poison his delight", so that Roderigo would be better placed to make his advances towards Desdemona.

In Act 2 scene 1, Iago's jealous intent towards Othello is so strong that he says, "Doth, like a poisonous mineral, gnaw my inwards". Hence, in Act 2 scene 3, Iago's vows to "pour this pestilence into his ear".

The most chilling use of the word poison uttered by Othello is when he contemplates killing Desdemona in Act 3 scene 3, "If there be cords or knives, Poison or fire ...".

Finally, in Act 4 scene 1, Othello's mind poisoned with jealous thoughts, decides to kill Desdemona in the bed that he thinks she has poisoned with her wanton lust.

"Get me some poison, Iago, this night.
I'll not expostulate with her, lest her body and beauty
Unprovide my mind again"

At the end of the play, in Act 5 scene 2, Lodovico makes plain to Iago,

"Look on the tragic loading of this bed
This is thy work
The object poisons sight"

IRONY

Shakespeare uses **irony** to help the audience understand the action, where the audience know more than the characters. Iago is the main character for the situational, verbal, and dramatic irony of the play.

The irony for Othello is that his greatness, respect, and love, are destroyed by an evil subordinate, hence the tragedy! Another irony, he dies by his own hand under armed guard!

The irony is that Iago believes he is in full control of events and his victims, but his downfall is the results of underestimating Emilia his wife, who exposes his devilish plans to all at the end of the play, and Roderigo who confirms his plans in a letter. Instead of victory, Iago is condemned to torture, and eventual death. A rich reward, appropriate for an evil doer!

Desdemona's irony is that instead of consummating her marriage in Cyprus, her marriage bed becomes her deathbed! It is not Desdemona's morals that are corrupted but Othello's!

TEXT AND EXPLANATION

The Shakespearian text is written in the left column, and the explanation and interpretation, in the right column.

Important quotes and phrases in the text are highlighted and reproduced in the explanation column for discussion, on the same page. Consequently, there is no need to turn pages!

A summary of each Act precedes the text and explanation to give an overall perspective of the events in the story.

ACT 1

SUMMARY

In scene 1

- The play opens with a conflict between Iago and Roderigo. The setting is a scene at night in Venice. Roderigo is irked with Iago for not fulfilling his promise of a marriage between him and Desdemona.
- Iago expresses his hatred for Othello who promoted an inexperienced soldier, Cassio instead of him.
- He reveals that he intends to seek revenge by means of faithful service to Othello.
- The pair go to Brabantio's house and wake him up to tell him of his daughter's elopement with Othello.
- He is furious and goes out to find her.

In scene 2

- Brabantio confronts Othello on the street and Othello is very cordial and asks that they put their weapons away and discuss the problem in a calm manner.
- Othello is not fazed by Brabantio's accusations, and he is prepared to face the consequences. He is convinced that his unblemished reputation as a soldier, his royal breeding and his mannerisms will hold him in good stead for Desdemona's hand in marriage.
- Cassio reports that Othello is wanted for a meeting of the Venetian council.
- Brabantio decides to go to the meeting himself to report Othello's treachery and discredit him.

In scene 3

- The Duke and the Senate are discussing the attack by the Turks on Cyprus. The Duke enlists Othello's help because of his great reputation as a soldier.
- Brabantio is impatient to air his concerns about his daughter's elopement. Othello and Desdemona confirm that she was also responsible for this elopement and that they love each other dearly.
- The Duke intervenes and he is satisfied that Othello is innocent of Brabantio's accusations of witchcraft and abduction and he asks Brabantio to reconcile himself to this union.
- Desdemona wishes to accompany her husband to Cyprus and Othello faithfully places her in Iago's care.
- Iago convinces Roderigo that he will somehow get Desdemona to fall in love with him.
- In his aside Iago reveals how he will set his deadly plan in motion.

Venice at night.
A Street

Enter
RODERIGO *and* IAGO

RODERIGO
Tush, never tell me! I take it much unkindly
That thou, Iago, who hast had my purse
As if the strings were thine, shouldst know of this.
IAGO
'Sblood, but you'll not hear me!
If ever I did dream of such a matter, abhor me!
RODERIGO
Thou toldst me thou didst hold him in thy hate.
IAGO
Despise me
If I do not. Three great ones of the city,
In personal suit to make me his lieutenant,
Off-capped to him; and, by the faith of man,
I know my price, I am worth no worse a place.
But he, as loving his own pride and purposes,
Evades them with a bombast circumstance,
Horribly stuffed with epithets of war,
And in conclusion,
Nonsuits my mediators. For "Certes," says he,
"I have already chose my officer."
And what was he?
Forsooth, a great arithmetician,
One Michael Cassio, a Florentine,
A fellow almost damned in a fair wife,
That never set a squadron in the field,
Nor the division of a battle knows
More than a spinster—unless the bookish theoric,
Wherein the togèd consuls can propose
As masterly as he. Mere prattle without practice
Is all his soldiership. But he, sir, had th' election;
And I, of whom his eyes had seen the proof
At Rhodes, at Cyprus, and on other grounds
Christened and heathen, must be beleed and calmed
By debitor and creditor. This counter-caster,
He, in good time, must his lieutenant be,
And I, God bless the mark, his Moorship's ancient.

Shakespeare opens this scene with a very strained conversation between Iago and Roderigo. Roderigo is in a very foul mood because Iago took his money,

"who hast had my purse
As if the strings were thine"

And didn't fulfil his promise to secure a marriage between Roderigo and Desdemona. Iago's meticulous use of language to manipulate and wriggle himself out of precarious situations is quite evident here,

"If ever I did dream of such a matter,
abhor me!"

Iago expresses his shock at these unusual turn of events – the marriage between Othello and Desdemona.

His repetition of the harsh language,

'abhor me' and 'Despise me'

gives the reader an inkling of his unsavoury character and Shakespeare sets the tone for us right at the outset of what to expect from Iago.

He expresses his deepest feelings of hate towards Othello for bypassing him for the coveted position of lieutenant.

Shakespeare uses dramatic irony here when he unravels Iago's thirst for revenge which we the audience is well aware of but the characters are oblivious of the terrible fate that is about to befall them.

TEXT ACT 1 scene 1

RODERIGO
By heaven, I rather would have been his hangman.
IAGO
Why, there's no remedy. 'Tis the curse of service.
Preferment goes by letter and affection,
And not by old gradation, where each second
Stood heir to th' first. Now, sir, be judge yourself
Whether I in any just term am affined
To love the Moor.
RODERIGO
I would not follow him, then.
IAGO
O, sir, content you.
I follow him to serve my turn upon him.
We cannot all be masters, nor all masters
Cannot be truly followed. You shall mark
Many a duteous and knee-crooking knave
That, doting on his own obsequious bondage,
Wears out his time, much like his master's ass,
For naught but provender,
And when he's old, cashiered.
Whip me such honest knaves! Others there are
Who, trimmed in forms and visages of duty,
Keep yet their hearts attending on themselves,
And, throwing but shows of service on their lords,
Do well thrive by them,
And when they have lined their coats,
Do themselves homage.
These fellows have some soul,
And such a one do I profess myself. For, sir,
It is as sure as you are Roderigo,
Were I the Moor I would not be Iago.
In following him, I follow but myself.
Heaven is my judge, not I for love and duty,
But seeming so for my peculiar end.
For when my outward action doth demonstrate
The native act and figure of my heart
In complement extern, 'tis not long after
But I will wear my heart upon my sleeve
For daws to peck at. I am not what I am.
RODERIGO
What a full fortune does the thick-lips owe
If he can carry 't thus!

EXPLANATION

The central theme of jealousy is a powerful motif which runs throughout the play. Here we witness Iago's professional jealousy of Cassio who he believes usurped his position of being lieutenant.

"Preferment goes by letter and affection."

Iago pacifies Roderigo into believing that he does not love Othello,

"Whether I in any just term am affined
To love the Moor."

Shakespeare creates a clash of private, professional and political ideals coupled with the themes of deception and jealousy and Iago as the driving force who reveals his villainy and motive for causing Othello harm,

"I follow him to serve my turn upon him."

Iago despises loyal servants who work hard for their masters and when they get old are terminated like his master's ass.

"when he's old, cashiered."

We see the theme of appearance verses reality when Iago says that he merely pretends to be a loyal servant, but in reality, he is only thinking about himself to achieve his own goals,

"not I for love and duty,
But seeming so For my peculiar end."

In act 1 scene 1 Othello is not mentioned by name but by the 'Moor' and 'thick lips' which are derogatory, stereotypical racist terms and shows a lack of respect for Othello.

Iago seem to possess a certain confidence and he seems to be directing the action with his contemptuous and egotistical behaviour.

He directs Roderigo to arouse Brabantio from his sleep.

IAGO
Call up her father.
Rouse him. Make after him, poison his delight,
Proclaim him in the streets; incense her kinsmen,
And, though he in a fertile climate dwell,
Plague him with flies. Though that his joy be joy,
Yet throw such chances of vexation on 't
As it may lose some colour.

RODERIGO
Here is her father's house. I'll call aloud.

IAGO
Do, with like timorous accent and dire yell
As when, by night and negligence, the fire
Is spied in populous cities.

RODERIGO
What ho, Brabantio! Signior Brabantio, ho!

IAGO
Awake! What ho, Brabantio! Thieves, thieves!
Look to your house, your daughter, and your bags!
Thieves, thieves!

Enter
BRABANTIO, *above.*

BRABANTIO
What is the reason of this terrible summons?
What is the matter there?

RODERIGO
Signior, is all your family within?

IAGO
Are your doors locked?

BRABANTIO
Why, wherefore ask you this?

IAGO
Zounds, sir, you're robbed. For shame, put on your gown!
Your heart is burst. You have lost half your soul.
Even now, now, very now, an old black ram
Is tupping your white ewe. Arise, arise!
Awake the snorting citizens with the bell,
Or else the devil will make a grandsire of you.
Arise, I say!

Shakespeare's use of short, snappy sentences which increases the pace and the urgency of the situation, suggests that Iago is relishing the thought of the mischief that he is about to cause.

The use of the metaphor,

"Plague him with flies."

can suggest Iago's corrupt and diseased mind, full of evil intentions.

Brabantio is furious at being disturbed and he castigates Roderigo for his behaviour.

We are confronted with a very indignant and vulgar Iago. His crudeness is shocking when he describes the physical, sexual union between Othello and Desdemona to that of animals.

Shakespeare's use of the animal imagery,

"an old black ram
Is tupping your white ewe."

The colour imagery 'black' and 'white', highlight the social and historical context of the play and it's racial innuendos.

Iago is very dramatic, and he very successfully manages to disrupt the peace and instigate chaos in the physical security of Brabantio's house.

He exploded a peaceful surrounding with his vile utterances. His action here foreshadows the chaos and mayhem he causes later which results In Desdemona's death. Shakespeare also uses biblical imagery associating Othello to the devil,

"the devil will make a grandsire of you."

TEXT ACT 1 scene 1

BRABANTIO
What, have you lost your wits?
RODERIGO
Most reverend signior, do you know my voice?
BRABANTIO
Not I. What are you?
RODERIGO
My name is Roderigo.
BRABANTIO
The worser welcome.
I have charged thee not to haunt about my doors.
In honest plainness thou hast heard me say
My daughter is not for thee. And now in madness,
Being full of supper and distemp'ring draughts,
Upon malicious bravery dost thou come
To start my quiet.
RODERIGO
Sir, sir, sir—
BRABANTIO
But thou must needs be sure
My spirit and my place have in them power
To make this bitter to thee.
RODERIGO
Patience, good sir.
BRABANTIO
What tell'st thou me of robbing?
This is Venice. My house is not a grange.
RODERIGO
Most grave Brabantio,
In simple and pure soul I come to you—
IAGO
Zounds, sir, you are one of those that will not serve God if the devil bid you. Because we come to do you service and you think we are ruffians, you'll have your daughter covered with a Barbary horse, you'll have your nephews neigh to you, you'll have coursers for cousins and jennets for Germans.
BRABANTIO
What profane wretch art thou?
IAGO
I am one, sir, that comes to tell you your daughter
And the Moor are now making the beast with two backs.
BRABANTIO
Thou art a villain.
IAGO
You are a sena**tor.**
BRABANTIO
This thou shalt answer. I know thee, Roderigo.

EXPLANATION

Iago is very manipulative in his choice of words to entice Brabantio.

"we come to do you service."

He uses an animal imagery, 'Barbary horse' Associating Othello to an animal.

Once again, we see his racist remarks and the negative, black stereotypes which were prevalent in Elizabethan society at the time. Venice had a more rigid class structure than England and the theme of class and racism is a common theme that runs throughout the play.

The Elizabethan audience had a very skewed view of unions between black and white and their prejudices are clearly depicted in the play.

Roderigo describes the Moor's sexuality in very crude terms suggesting lust and uncanny sexual behaviour.

RODERIGO

Sir, I will answer anything. But I beseech you,
If 't be your pleasure and most wise consent—
As partly I find it is—that your fair daughter,
At this odd-even and dull watch o' th' night,
Transported with no worse nor better guard
But with a knave of common hire, a gondolier,
To the gross clasps of a lascivious Moor:
If this be known to you, and your allowance,
We then have done you bold and saucy wrongs.
But if you know not this, my manners tell me
We have your wrong rebuke. Do not believe
That from the sense of all civility
I thus would play and trifle with your Reverence.
Your daughter, if you have not given her leave,
I say again, hath made a gross revolt,
Tying her duty, beauty, wit, and fortunes
In an extravagant and wheeling stranger
Of here and everywhere. Straight satisfy yourself.
If she be in her chamber or your house,
Let loose on me the justice of the state
For thus deluding you.

BRABANTIO

Strike on the tinder, ho!
Give me a taper. Call up all my people!
This accident is not unlike my dream.
Belief of it oppresses me already.
Light, I say, light!

BRABANTIO ***exits***

IAGO, *to Roderigo*

Farewell, for I must leave you.
It seems not meet nor wholesome to my place
To be producted, as if I stay I shall,
Against the Moor. For I do know the state,
However this may gall him with some check,
Cannot with safety cast him, for he's embarked
With such loud reason to the Cyprus wars,
Which even now stands in act, that, for their souls,
Another of his fathom they have none
To lead their business. In which regard,
Though I do hate him as I do hell pains,
Yet, for necessity of present life,
I must show out a flag and sign of love.
Which is indeed but sign. That you shall surely find
him,
Lead to the Sagittary the raisèd search,
And there will I be with him. So, farewell.

IAGO ***exits***

It was unnatural because of the glaring racial barriers that existed between the two and all the characters in Act 1 scene 1 voiced their negative opinions of it.

"But with a knave of common hire."

Roderigo reveals his very negative view of Desdemona's elopement to Brabantio.

He relays in very measured tones and in a very bawdy manner how Desdemona is now in,

"the gross clasps of a lascivious Moor."

He also hints at the disparity in social positions between Desdemona and the Moor. One can also claim that there is a reversal of the normal order in this match.

Roderigo's demeanour is very similar to Iago's, because he is very persuasive and by his choice of words,

"trifle with your Reverence."

Was able to captivate Brabantio's attention because he became furious and this fury is detected in his short, snappy utterances,

"Give me a taper. Call up my people!"

suggesting his rising temper.
His fury is understandable because he is a man of status, and his social position is now threatened. Iago is manipulative because we have already gaged that he hates the Moor, yet he praises his accolades,

"Another of his fathom they have none."

However, we see the theme of appearance versus reality where Iago is pretending to love the Moor,

"I must show out a flag and sign of love."

A look at the historical context is imperative here because the war between Venice and Cyprus can be mirrored with the raging war between Brabantio, his daughter and the Moor.

Enter
BRABANTIO *in his nightgown,*
with Servants and Torches.

BRABANTIO
It is too true an evil. Gone she is,
And what's to come of my despisèd time
Is naught but bitterness.—Now, Roderigo,
Where didst thou see her?—O, unhappy girl!—
With the Moor, sayst thou?—Who would be a father -
How didst thou know 'twas she?—O, she deceives me
Past thought!—What said she to you?—Get more
tapers.
Raise all my kindred.—Are they married, think you?

RODERIGO
Truly, I think they are.

BRABANTIO
O heaven! How got she out? O treason of the blood!
Fathers, from hence trust not your daughters' minds
By what you see them act.—Is there not charms
By which the property of youth and maidhood
May be abused? Have you not read, Roderigo,
Of some such thing?

RODERIGO
Yes, sir, I have indeed.

BRABANTIO
Call up my brother.—O, would you had had her!—
Some one way, some another.—Do you know
Where we may apprehend her and the Moor?

RODERIGO
I think I can discover him, if you please
To get good guard and go along with me.

BRABANTIO
Pray you lead on. At every house I'll call.
I may command at most.—Get weapons, ho!
And raise some special officers of night.
On, good Roderigo. I will deserve your pains.

THERY *exit*

We have to look at the themes of social issues because the social order has been disrupted when Desdemona crossed the racial barrier and married a black man which was frowned upon at that time.

Brabantio's speech seems to be very fragmented here with the repetition of hyphens and question marks suggesting his exasperation, dilemma and his disgust,

"O treason of the blood!"

One can infer that Desdemona betrayed the pure blood line by marrying a black man. Brabantio belonged to the upper crust of Venice's society where morals, prosperity and power are revered.

In the Elizabethan era, women were seen as second-class citizens and were controlled by the dominant male. Brabantio thinks that Desdemona is his property, and he has to make decisions for her.

"By which the property of youth and
maidhood May be abused."

This is ironical because Brabantio makes reference to property which he associates to Desdemona's youth and something that he owns.

Now Brabantio regrets having turned away Roderigo's proposal of marriage to Desdemona.

To Brabantio it is erratic behaviour, clearly visible by the many actions he proposes to undertake,

"apprehend her and the Moor"

and commands,

"Get weapons, ho!"

He is clearly in desperation to salvage the situation and his desperate acts are not in sync with his social position where he commands his servants but here there is a reversal of roles similar to the marriage of the Moor and Desdemona.

Another Street

Enter
OTHELLO, IAGO,
and Attendants with Torches

IAGO
Though in the trade of war I have slain men,
Yet do I hold it very stuff o' th' conscience
To do no contrived murder. I lack iniquity
Sometimes to do me service. Nine or ten times
I had thought t' have yerked him here under the rib.

OTHELLO
'Tis better as it is.

IAGO
Nay, but he prated
And spoke such scurvy and provoking terms
Against your Honour,
That with the little godliness I have
I did full hard forbear him. But I pray you, sir,
Are you fast married? Be assured of this,
That the magnifico is much beloved,
And hath in his effect a voice potential
As double as the Duke's. He will divorce you
Or put upon you what restraint or grievance
The law (with all his might to enforce it on)
Will give him cable.

OTHELLO
Let him do his spite.
My services which I have done the signiory
Shall out-tongue his complaints. 'Tis yet to know
(Which, when I know that boasting is an honour,
I shall promulgate) I fetch my life and being
From men of royal siege, and my demerits
May speak unbonneted to as proud a fortune
As this that I have reached. For know, Iago,
But that I love the gentle Desdemona,
I would not my unhoused free condition
Put into circumscription and confine
For the sea's worth. But look, what lights come yond?

Iago's hypocrisy astounds the reader. He speaks with a silver tongue but in fact his words are a double-edged sword to make mischief. The theme of appearance versus reality surfaces again. He says that,

"I lack iniquity
Sometimes to do me service."

His self-deprecating behaviour is hilarious because he is full of iniquity and says that he has a conscience and would not commit murder.

"th' conscience
To do no contrived murder"

yet we are aware that his despicable actions contribute to the Death of Desdemona. He threatens Othello by saying that Brabantio can have his marriage annulled if it wasn't consummated and slyly enquiries if it has.

We are now introduced to Othello whose name is already besmirched and his reputation dragged to the gutter by Iago. Yet Iago now disgracefully changed his tune, and he tells Othello that Brabantio,

"spoke such scurvy and provoking terms
Against your Honour "

Scurvy is a disease that sailors suffered because of a lack of vitamin C. Iago associates Brabantio's rantings to that of the dreaded disease to create a negative reaction in Othello. But Othello displays a certain calm, and he speaks in a very measured tone and his self-confidence is admirable. He is sure that his accolades of being a celebrated soldier who led armies to war and who is a favourite of the state and his deep and sincere love for Desdemona will restore his dignity and bail him out from this tangled web of lies that Iago is ensnaring him into.

"My services which I have done the signiory
shall out-tongue his complaints."

IAGO
Those are the raised father and his friends.
You were best go in.
OTHELLO
Not I. I must be found.
My parts, my title, and my perfect soul
Shall manifest me rightly. Is it they?
IAGO
By Janus, I think no.

Enter
CASSIO, *with Officers, and Torches.*

OTHELLO
The servants of the Duke and my lieutenant!
The goodness of the night upon you, friends.
What is the news?
CASSIO
The Duke does greet you, general,
And he requires your haste-post-haste appearance,
Even on the instant.
OTHELLO
What is the matter, think you?
CASSIO
Something from Cyprus, as I may divine.
It is a business of some heat. The galleys
Have sent a dozen sequent messengers
This very night at one another's heels,
And many of the Consuls, raised and met,
Are at the Duke's already. You have been hotly
called for.
When, being not at your lodging to be found,
The Senate hath sent about three several quests
To search you out.
OTHELLO
'Tis well I am found by you.
I will but spend a word here in the house
And go with you.
HE *exits*

CASSIO
Ancient, what makes he here?
IAGO
Faith, he tonight hath boarded a land carrack.
If it prove lawful prize, he's made forever.

Othello is courageous and insists that he has to be found and he will face his problems like a man.

"Not I. I must be found."

Othello speaks in blank verse very politely which people from the upper echelons of society use, whereas people from the lower socialist class spoke in prose.

We have to take note of the distinct gap between the social classes in Elizabethan times. Iago's speeches are riddled with both prose and verse maybe to master his art of manipulation because he is the 'master chameleon of speech'.

Another view to adopt is that Iago is a humble servant and ordinary soldier but yearns to have the status of the upper class. In Act 1 scene 1 line 40, he remarks that

"Preferment goes by letter and affection."

Meaning that Cassio was preferred for the position of lieutenant because of his social status instead of Iago.

The Duke requested Othello's presence and it's obvious that he is revered for his services because the Senate sent out three search parties to find him.

"You have been hotly called for."

Iago's contemptuous behaviour rears its ugly head once again. He was the architect of all the trouble, he ignited the fire and spurred Brabantio into action.

TEXT ACT 1 scene 2

CASSIO
I do not understand.
IAGO
He's married.
CASSIO
To who?
IAGO
Marry, to—

***Re-enter* OTHELLO**

Come, captain, will you go?
OTHELLO
Have with you.
CASSIO
Here comes another troop to seek for you.

Enter
BRABANTIO, RODERIGO,
with Officers, and Torches and weapons.

IAGO
It is Brabantio. General, be advised,
He comes to bad intent.
OTHELLO
Holla, stand there!
RODERIGO
Signior, it is the Moor.
BRABANTIO
Down with him, thief!

THEY *draw their swords.*

IAGO
You, Roderigo! Come, sir, I am for you.
OTHELLO
Keep up your bright swords, for the dew will rust them
Good signior, you shall more command with years
Than with your weapons.

EXPLANATION

Now he turns the tables, and he tells Othello that Brabantio's intent is bad, and he is coming to harm him, and Brabantio is livid, and he calls Othello a 'thief'.

Brabantio calls Othello a thief because he says he stole his daughter, and he looks at his daughter as his possession or property because possessions and property are generally stolen so Brabantio indirectly associates his daughter to an inanimate object having no status or say in her choices hence was the status of women in the Elizabethan era.

Othello is very stoic, and he wisely advises Brabantio that he shouldn't fight at his age but to try to be civil and iron out their problems with wit and negotiations.

A clear depiction of the theme of conflict between Brabantio and Othello surfaces here. Brabantio hurls verbal abuse and he dehumanises Othello.

Thus far we marvel at Othello's stoicism and quiet dignity. Yet he is a black man caught up in the whirlwind of an aristocratic world of racist, vile individuals. The repetition of the adjective, 'thief' suggests that Desdemona was an unwilling participant in this union.

The Elizabethan audience believed in witchcraft, and they associated black people to the devil and witchcraft as seen in Brabantio's rantings.

BRABANTIO

O, thou foul thief, where hast thou stowed my daughter?
Damned as thou art, thou hast enchanted her!
For I'll refer me to all things of sense,
If she in chains of magic were not bound,
Whether a maid so tender, fair, and happy,
So opposite to marriage that she shunned
The wealthy curled darlings of our nation,
Would ever have, t' incur a general mock,
Run from her guardage to the sooty bosom
Of such a thing as thou—to fear, not to delight!
Judge me the world, if 'tis not gross in sense
That thou hast practiced on her with foul charms,
Abused her delicate youth with drugs or minerals
That weakens motion. I'll have 't disputed on.
'Tis probable, and palpable to thinking.
I therefore apprehend and do attach thee
For an abuser of the world, a practicer
Of arts inhibited and out of warrant. —
Lay hold upon him. If he do resist,
Subdue him at his peril.

OTHELLO

Hold your hands,
Both you of my inclining and the rest.
Were it my cue to fight, I should have known it
Without a prompter. —Whither will you that I go
To answer this your charge?

BRABANTIO

To prison, till fit time
Of law and course of direct session
Call thee to answer.

OTHELLO

What if I do obey?
How may the Duke be therewith satisfied,
Whose messengers are here about my side,
Upon some present business of the state,
To bring me to him?

OFFICER

'Tis true, most worthy signior.
The Duke's in council, and your noble self
I am sure is sent for.

BRABANTIO

How? The Duke in council?
In this time of the night? Bring him away;
Mine's not an idle cause. The Duke himself,
Or any of my brothers of the state,
Cannot but feel this wrong as 'twere their own.
For if such actions may have passage free,
Bond slaves and pagans shall our statesmen be.

THEY ***exit***

He accuses Othello of using witchcraft to seduce his daughter. He uses a prison imagery saying that she was chained and bound by magic,

"If she in chains of magic were not bound"

Brabantio continues to hurl demeaning racial slurs at Othello,

"Run from her guardage to the sooty bosom"

The adjective 'sooty' is associated to black and dirty.

Brabantio verbally abuses Othello with a rather caustic tone, and he is furious that his daughter married a black man.

His social status, dignity and reputation is threatened because such a union between black and white was frowned upon.

He accuses Othello of drugging and kidnapping his daughter.

"Abused her delicate youth with drugs"

Brabantio wants Othello arrested.

Othello is level-headed and strong, and he tries to diffuse an extremely volatile situation.

"How may the Duke be therewith satisfied"

Brabantio speaks very harshly to him and his erratic behaviour would have led to a serious scuffle, but Othello was very authoritative and firm and sought an amicable solution to the problem where Brabantio decides to go to the council meeting and inform the senators of Othello's treacherous behaviour.

TEXT ACT 1 scene 3

A Council Chamber

Enter
Duke, Senators, *and* Officers

DUKE, *reading a paper*
There's no composition in these news
That gives them credit.
FIRST SENATOR, *reading a paper*
Indeed, they are disproportioned.
My letters say a hundred and seven galleys.
DUKE
And mine, a hundred forty.
SECOND SENATOR, *reading a paper*
And mine, two hundred.
But though they jump not on a just account
As in these cases, where the aim reports
'Tis oft with difference, yet do they all confirm
A Turkish fleet and bearing up to Cyprus.
DUKE
Nay, it is possible enough to judgment.
I do not so secure me in the error,
But the main article I do approve
In fearful sense.
SAILOR, *within*
What ho, what ho, what ho!

***Enter* Sailor**

OFFICER
A messenger from the galleys.
DUKE
Now, what's the business?
SAILOR
The Turkish preparation makes for Rhodes.
So was I bid report here to the state
By Signior Angelo.
HE *exits*
DUKE
How say you by this change?
FIRST SENATOR
This cannot be,
By no assay of reason. 'Tis a pageant,
To keep us in false gaze. When we consider
Th' importancy of Cyprus to the Turk,
And let ourselves again but understand
That, as it more concerns the Turk than Rhodes,
So may he with more facile question bear it,
For that it stands not in such warlike brace,
But altogether lacks th' abilities
That Rhodes is dressed in. if we make thought of this
We must not think the Turk is so unskilful
To leave that latest which concerns him first,
Neglecting an attempt of ease and gain
To wake and wage a danger profitless.

EXPLANATION

There are conflicting wars raging here-the historical, between the Turks and Cyprus and the hierarchical social structure between Brabantio and Othello and between love and war.

The Duke and the two senators are discussing the inconsistencies in their reports. One can draw a parallel to the inconsistencies of the marriage between Othello and Desdemona and the social hierarchies between Othello and Brabantio.

The senator said that there is a confirmation that a Turkish fleet is approaching Cyprus.

It's important to note not only the physical conflicts but also the mental conflicts

For example, Iago has a conflict of interest because he was side-stepped for the job as lieutenant, and he is bent on taking revenge.

A sailor enters and announces that there has been an error and that the Turkish fleet is heading for Rhodes and not for Cyprus.

The Duke and the senator are surprised, and they discuss this sudden change. They believe that a trick has been played to mislead them,

"Tis a pageant,
To keep us in false gaze."

The Duke reassures the senator that the Turks are not headed for Rhodes.

The Senator says that Cyprus is very important to the Turks and we must not underestimate the Turks into thinking that they would procrastinate and leave what is important and place emphasis on profit less endeavours because they have the ability to capture Cyprus very easily.

"For that it stands not in such warlike brace,"

DUKE
Nay, in all confidence, he's not for Rhodes.
OFFICER
Here is more news.

***Enter a* MESSENGER**

MESSENGER
The Ottomites, Reverend and Gracious,
Steering with due course toward the isle of Rhodes,
Have there injointed them with an after fleet.
FIRST SENATOR
Ay, so I thought. How many, as you guess?
MESSENGER
Of thirty sail; and now they do restem
Their backward course, bearing with frank appearance
Their purposes toward Cyprus. Signior Montano,
Your trusty and most valiant servitor,
With his free duty recommends you thus,
And prays you to believe him.
HE *exits*

DUKE
'Tis certain, then, for Cyprus.
Marcus Luccicos, is not he in town?
FIRST SENATOR
He's now in Florence.
DUKE
Write from us to him.
Post-post-haste. Dispatch.
FIRST SENATOR
Here comes Brabantio and the valiant Moor.

Enter
BRABANTIO, OTHELLO, CASSIO,
IAGO, RODERIGO, *and* officers

DUKE
Valiant Othello, we must straight employ you
Against the general enemy Ottoman.
***To* Brabantio.**
I did not see you. Welcome, gentle signior.
We lacked your counsel and your help tonight.
BRABANTIO
So did I yours. Good your Grace, pardon me.
Neither my place nor aught I heard of business
Hath raised me from my bed, nor doth the general care
Take hold on me, for my particular grief
Is of so floodgate and o'erbearing nature
That it engluts and swallows other sorrows
And it is still itself.

The messenger brings news that 30 ships are heading for Cyprus. They have turned around and are heading for Cyprus and he says that Signior Montano a most trusted servant sends this information.

The Duke enquires after Marcus Luccicos and learns that he is still in Florence and the Duke is desperate to contact him to help in the war effort.

"Post - post -haste. Dispatch."

The senator sees Othello enter with Brabantio and he greets Othello very gallantly and very cordially makes reference to his bravery,

"Here comes Brabantio and the valiant
Moor."

The repetition of the adjective 'valiant' by the duke suggests that the duke had the utmost respect for Othello as a soldier. He tells Othello that he must dispatch him immediately to fight the Turks.

The Duke then notices Brabantio and tells him that they missed his wisdom and could have done with some of his help tonight.

Brabantio told him that it wasn't war or business that aroused him from his sleep and that it is something more sinister and urgent.

In his grief he gives us an imagery of his pain pouring out through the flood gates and that it is so gut-wrenching that no other sorrow can overpower it,

"swallows other sorrows."

TEXT ACT 1 scene 3

DUKE
Why, what's the matter?
BRABANTIO
My daughter! O, my daughter!
FIRST SENATOR
Dead?
BRABANTIO
Ay, to me.
She is abused, stol'n from me, and corrupted
By spells and medicines bought of mountebanks.
For nature so prepost'rously to err—
Being not deficient, blind, or lame of sense—
Sans witchcraft could not.
DUKE
Whoe'er he be that in this foul proceeding
Hath thus beguiled your daughter of herself
And you of her, the bloody book of law
You shall yourself read in the bitter letter,
After your own sense, yea, though our proper son
Stood in your action.
BRABANTIO
Humbly I thank your Grace.
Here is the man—this Moor, whom now it seems
Your special mandate for the state affairs
Hath hither brought.
ALL
We are very sorry for 't.
DUKE, *to Othello*
What, in your own part, can you say to this?
BRABANTIO
Nothing, but this is so.
OTHELLO
Most potent, grave, and reverend signiors,
My very noble and approved good masters:
That I have ta'en away this old man's daughter,
It is most true; true I have married her.
The very head and front of my offending
Hath this extent, no more. Rude am I in my speech,
And little blessed with the soft phrase of peace,
For since these arms of mine had seven years' pith,
Till now some nine moons wasted, they have used
Their dearest action in the tented field,
And little of this great world can I speak
More than pertains to feats of broil and battle.
And therefore little shall I grace my cause
In speaking for myself. Yet, by your gracious
patience,
I will a round unvarnished tale deliver
Of my whole course of love—
what drugs, what charms,
What conjuration, and what mighty magic
For such proceeding I am charged withal
I won his daughter.

EXPLANATION

He blurts out very emotionally,

"My daughter! O, my daughter!"

Note the use of the repetition 'daughter' suggesting his untold pain.

Brabantio rants about how she was stolen and corrupted by witchcraft and the duke enquires who is responsible for this foul deed and promises him that the long arm of the law will deal with the perpetrator.

Brabantio tells the Duke that Othello is responsible for the foul deed.

We should notice how these men from the higher social hierarchy address Othello as the Moor – a native of North African, decent.

One can connote that it signifies a certain level of disrespect and drawing attention to the fact that he is a foreigner.

In the sixteenth century Christians were suspicious of the Moors. They attacked their religious beliefs labelling them heathens.

We will also look at the theme of xenophobia when we consider Iago being sidestepped for the job as lieutenant by the Moor who is a foreigner hence Iago's hate for the Moor.

Othello took responsibility for his actions and acknowledges that he took Desdemona and married her and that's his only offense.

Othello lacks confidence in his speech, maybe it's because of his social status.

"Rude am I in my speech,"

He says that his life was dedicated to fighting and he very eloquently explains that he had no experience with women, but their love is genuine and that there's a deep bond between them.

Othello emphasised that,

"I won his daughter."

BRABANTIO
A maiden never bold,
Of spirit so still and quiet that her motion
Blushed at herself. And she, in spite of nature,
Of years, of country, credit, everything,
To fall in love with what she feared to look on!
It is a judgment maimed and most imperfect
That will confess perfection so could err
Against all rules of nature, and must be driven
To find out practices of cunning hell
Why this should be. I therefore vouch again
That with some mixtures powerful o'er the blood,
Or with some dram conjured to this effect,
He wrought upon her.

DUKE
To vouch this is no proof
Without more wider and more overt test
Than these thin habits and poor likelihoods
Of modern seeming do prefer against him.

FIRST SENATOR
But, Othello, speak:
Did you by indirect and forced courses
Subdue and poison this young maid's affections?
Or came it by request, and such fair question
As soul to soul affordeth?

OTHELLO
I do beseech you,
Send for the lady to the Sagittary
And let her speak of me before her father.
If you do find me foul in her report,
The trust, the office I do hold of you,
Not only take away, but let your sentence
Even fall upon my life.

DUKE
Fetch Desdemona hither.

OTHELLO
Ancient, conduct them. You best know the place.

IAGO *and* **Attendants** ***exit***

And till she come, as truly as to heaven
I do confess the vices of my blood,
So justly to your grave ears I'll present
How I did thrive in this fair lady's love,
And she in mine.

DUKE
Say it, Othello.

And that he is not guilty of using witchcraft and magic that he is accused of.

Brabantio's racial prejudices are quite evident here because he is insisting that this is a

"judgement maimed and most imperfect."

"Against all rules of nature."

Brabantio is adamant that Othello used witchcraft to entice Desdemona.

Othello asks for Desdemona to be brought in to bear witness to the truth and refute this ludicrous accusation that Brabantio is levelling against her husband.

If she besmirches my character, then you can put me to death.

"If you do find me foul in her report"

Then

"let your sentence
Even fall upon my life"

Othello instructs Iago to bring Desdemona in and in the meantime, he promises to confess to his sins. He said that he will be as truthful as possible to tell them how he fell in love with Desdemona.

Her father was very cordial to him and invited him over to his house and questioned him about his life.

OTHELLO

Her father loved me, oft invited me,
Still questioned me the story of my life
From year to year—the battles, sieges, fortunes
That I have passed.
I ran it through, even from my boyish days
To th' very moment that he bade me tell it,
Wherein I spoke of most disastrous chances:
Of moving accidents by flood and field,
Of hairbreadth 'scapes i' th' imminent deadly breach
Of being taken by the insolent foe
And sold to slavery, of my redemption thence,
And portance in my traveler's history,
Wherein of antres vast and deserts idle,
Rough quarries, rocks, and hills whose heads
touch heaven,
It was my hint to speak—such was my process—
And of the cannibals that each other eat,
The Anthropophagi, and men whose heads
Do grow beneath their shoulders.
These things to hear
Would Desdemona seriously incline.
But still the house affairs would draw her thence,
Which ever as she could with haste dispatch
She'd come again, and with a greedy ear
Devour up my discourse. Which I, observing,
Took once a pliant hour, and found good means
To draw from her a prayer of earnest heart
That I would all my pilgrimage dilate,
Whereof by parcels she had something heard,
But not intentively. I did consent,
And often did beguile her of her tears
When I did speak of some distressful stroke
That my youth suffered. My story being done,
She gave me for my pains a world of sighs.
She swore, in faith, 'twas strange, 'twas passing
strange,
'Twas pitiful, 'twas wondrous pitiful.
She wished she had not heard it, yet she wished
That heaven had made her such a man.
She thanked me,
And bade me, if I had a friend that loved her,
I should but teach him how to tell my story,
And that would woo her. Upon this hint I spake.
She loved me for the dangers I had passed,
And I loved her that she did pity them.
This only is the witchcraft I have used.
Here comes the lady. Let her witness it.

Enter
DESDEMONA, IAGO, *Attendants*

He relayed to him the wonders of his battles, his dangerous adventures, hair-raising escapades and how he was sold to slavery and how he managed to free himself.

"sold to slavery, of my redemption thence"

He spoke about cannibals eating each other, and men whose heads grew below their shoulders.

"And of the cannibals that each other eat"

These stories mesmerised Desdemona and captured her interest.

We have to juxtapose Brabantio's politeness to Othello here to that of his present vile, unsavoury accusations and hatred towards him.

His speeches were full of racial slurs. One can assume that it was very well to accept Othello from a distance, but once Brabantio learnt that Othello was bold enough to cross the racial barriers and the rigid, hierarchical social structure, he was livid.

He called the union between Othello and Desdemona, in effect, 'a slur against nature'.

It's obvious that his love for Othello was superficial.

Desdemona, Othello says relished in his storytelling, and it fascinated her so much that she gave him,

"a world of sighs"

She wished that she had not heard it because she became so emotional and she also hoped ironically that,

"heaven had made her such a man."

We can see a contrast here between Desdemona's view of her relationship with Othello to that of her father's, who called the union in Act 1 scene 3 line 70,

"For nature so prepost'rously to err-"

TEXT ACT 1 scene 3

DUKE
I think this tale would win my daughter, too.
Good Brabantio,
Take up this mangled matter at the best.
Men do their broken weapons rather use
Than their bare hands.

BRABANTIO
I pray you hear her speak.
If she confess that she was half the wooer,
Destruction on my head if my bad blame
Light on the man.—Come hither, gentle mistress.
Do you perceive in all this noble company
Where most you owe obedience?

DESDEMONA
My noble father,
I do perceive here a divided duty.
To you I am bound for life and education.
My life and education both do learn me
How to respect you. You are the lord of duty.
I am hitherto your daughter. But here's my
husband.
And so much duty as my mother showed
To you, preferring you before her father,
So much I challenge that I may profess
Due to the Moor my lord.

BRABANTIO
God be with you! I have done.
Please it your Grace, on to the state affairs.
I had rather to adopt a child than get it.—
Come hither, Moor.
I here do give thee that with all my heart
Which, but thou hast already, with all my heart
I would keep from thee.—For your sake, jewel,
I am glad at soul I have no other child,
For thy escape would teach me tyranny,
To hang clogs on them.—I have done, my lord.

DUKE
Let me speak like yourself and lay a sentence,
Which as a grise or step may help these lovers
Into your favour.
When remedies are past, the griefs are ended
By seeing the worst, which late on hopes depended.
To mourn a mischief that is past and gone
Is the next way to draw new mischief on.
What cannot be preserved when fortune takes,
Patience her injury a mock'ry makes.
The robbed that smiles steals something
from the thief;
He robs himself that spends a bootless grief.

EXPLANATION

We see an over-confident Brabantio who thinks that he was justified in his accusations.

Shakespeare creates tension here because the audience is eager to see Desdemona's and her father's reactions. The action has now reached a crescendo. The Duke uses beautiful imagery. He refers to this conflict as a

"mangled matter"

broken situation and he urges Brabantio to make the best of this situation. He goes on to say that,

"Men do their broken weapons rather use
than their bare hands."

He says it's better to accept the situation by using the broken tools referring to the Moor. Society was Patriarchal where men ran all the institutions. Strict social hierarchies imposed stringent rules on women to protect the honour of their families.

Desdemona is the victim of such a rigid imposition and her character is scrutinised because she did the unthinkable by eloping with a black man, infuriating her father because his honour was besmirched.

She acted completely against the norms of Elizabethan women when she boldly tells her father that she is bound to him for her education and life, but her loyalty lies with her husband. She was also very vocal when she refuses to stay with her father and insists on accompanying her husband.

Her father resigned himself to accepting this marriage and was forced to give it his blessings.

The Duke gives some great advice for Brabantio to accept the lovers and to make the most of the situation instead of lamenting it, which would prove to be futile.

"He robs himself that spends a bootless
grief"

TEXT ACT 1 scene 3

BRABANTIO
So let the Turk of Cyprus us beguile,
We lose it not so long as we can smile.
He bears the sentence well that nothing bears
But the free comfort which from thence he hears;
But he bears both the sentence and the sorrow
That, to pay grief, must of poor patience borrow.
These sentences to sugar or to gall,
Being strong on both sides, are equivocal.
But words are words. I never yet did hear
That the bruised heart was piercèd through the ear.
I humbly beseech you, proceed to th' affairs of state.

DUKE
The Turk with a most mighty preparation makes for Cyprus. Othello, the fortitude of the place is best known to you. And though we have there a substitute of most allowed sufficiency, yet opinion, a sovereign mistress of effects, throws a more safer voice on you. You must therefore be content to slubber the gloss of your new fortunes with this more stubborn and boist'rous expedition.

OTHELLO
The tyrant custom, most grave senators,
Hath made the flinty and steel couch of war
My thrice-driven bed of down. I do agnize
A natural and prompt alacrity
I find in hardness, and do undertake
This present wars against the Ottomites.
Most humbly, therefore, bending to your state,
I crave fit disposition for my wife,
Due reference of place and exhibition,
With such accommodation and besort
As levels with her breeding.

DUKE
Why, at her father's.

BRABANTIO
I will not have it so.

OTHELLO
Nor I.

DESDEMONA
Nor would I there reside
To put my father in impatient thoughts
By being in his eye. Most gracious duke,
To my unfolding lend your prosperous ear
And let me find a charter in your voice
T' assist my simpleness.

DUKE
What would you, Desdemona?

EXPLANATION

A very irate Brabantio is clearly not impressed with this advice, so he hits back.

He merges the historical and the social contexts of the play. He draws a parallel between the theft of his daughter to that of the theft of Cyprus by the Turks.

He challenges the Duke on this illogical advice for him to smile and accept this marriage.

"So let the Turk of Cyprus us beguile,
We lose it not so long as we can smile."

Would the Duke do the same?

The Duke seems to be enamoured by Othello's military prowess. He is confident that Othello will have more success to defend Cyprus because he is familiar with the place.

Although they have a very capable soldier the Duke has more faith in Othello's expertise. He urges Othello to forsake his marital pleasures for now and undertake this dangerous task.

Othello makes use of cold, hard imagery,

"flinty and steel"
"hardness"

He says that he is accustomed to the hardships of military life which has rendered him cold and distant. This can foreshadow for later in the play when this coldness surfaces, and he kills his wife Desdemona. He requests that appropriate arrangements be made for his wife according to her status.

"I crave fit disposition for my wife"

She was also forthright in refusing to stay with her father saying that she did not wish to upset him.

"Nor would I there reside
To put my father in impatient thoughts"

saying that nature had made a big mistake to sanction this union between these two.

TEXT ACT 1 scene 3

DESDEMONA

That I love the Moor to live with him
My downright violence and storm of fortunes
May trumpet to the world. My heart's subdued
Even to the very quality of my lord.
I saw Othello's visage in his mind,
And to his honours and his valiant parts
Did I my soul and fortunes consecrate.
So that, dear lords, if I be left behind,
A moth of peace, and he go to the war,
The rites for why I love him are bereft me
And I a heavy interim shall support
By his dear absence. Let me go with him.

OTHELLO

Let her have your voice.
Vouch with me, heaven, I therefore beg it not
To please the palate of my appetite,
Nor to comply with heat the young affects
In me defunct and proper satisfaction,
But to be free and bounteous to her mind.
And heaven defend your good souls that you think
I will your serious and great business scant
For she is with me. No, when light-winged toys
Of feathered Cupid seel with wanton dullness
My speculative and officed instruments,
That my disports corrupt and taint my business,
Let housewives make a skillet of my helm,
And all indign and base adversities
Make head against my estimation.

DUKE

Be it as you shall privately determine,
Either for her stay or going. Th' affair cries haste,
And speed must answer it.

FIRST SENATOR

You must away tonight.

OTHELLO

With all my heart.

DUKE

At nine i' th' morning here we'll meet again.
Othello, leave some officer behind
And he shall our commission bring to you,
With such things else of quality and respect
As doth import you.

OTHELLO

So please your Grace, my ancient.
A man he is of honesty and trust.
To his conveyance I assign my wife,
With what else needful your good Grace shall think
To be sent after me.

EXPLANATION

She expresses her feelings of love for Othello and wishes to stay with him.

"And I a heavy interim shall support by his dear absence."

There is a stark contrast between Brabantio's description of his daughter in Act 1 scene 3 line 106,

'a maiden never bold'

to that of Othello's, Act 1 scene 3 line

'half the wooer'

Her father paints a picture of her as being the,
'damsel in distress'

Whilst Othello describes how she showed intense interest in him and practically started this relationship.

He said that he doesn't want her to accompany him for physical pleasure but to satisfy her mind.

"But to be free and bounteous to her mind."

He adds that he is a dedicated soldier and that it must not be mistaken that he will neglect his duties by her presence,

"I will your serious and great business scant
For she is with me"

The Duke is unconcerned whether Desdemona stays or goes. He expresses his concerns about the urgency of the matter and urges Othello to leave quickly.

The Duke confirms that he will receive his orders in the morning. We see a very naïve and gullible Othello because he says that his ensign is,

"A man he is of honesty and trust."

And that he will place his wife in his capable hands. It is ironical because Iago is nothing but honest and trustworthy.

DUKE
Let it be so. Good night to everyone.
to Brabantio.
And, noble signior,
If virtue no delighted beauty lack,
Your son-in-law is far more fair than black.

FIRST SENATOR
Adieu, brave Moor, use Desdemona well.

BRABANTIO
Look to her, Moor, if thou hast eyes to see.
She has deceived her father and may do thee.

HE *exits*

OTHELLO
My life upon her faith!

DUKE, SENATORS, CASSIO, *and* OFFICERS *exit*

Honest Iago,
My Desdemona must I leave to thee.
I prithee let thy wife attend on her,
And bring them after in the best advantage.—
Come, Desdemona, I have but an hour
Of love, of worldly matters, and direction
To spend with thee. We must obey the time.

OTHELLO *and* DESDEMONA *exit*

RODERIGO
Iago—

IAGO
What sayst thou, noble heart?

RODERIGO
What will I do, think'st thou?

IAGO
Why, go to bed and sleep.

RODERIGO
I will incontinently drown myself.

IAGO
If thou dost, I shall never love thee after.
Why, thou silly gentleman!

RODERIGO
It is silliness to live, when to live is torment,
And then have we a prescription to die
When death is our physician.

IAGO
O, villainous! I have looked upon the world for four times seven years, and since I could distinguish betwixt a benefit and an injury, I never found man that knew how to love himself. Ere I would say I would drown myself for the love of a guinea hen, I would change my humanity with a baboon.

RODERIGO
What should I do? I confess it is my shame to be so fond, but it is not in my virtue to amend it.

Shakespeare creates a lot of suspense and tension here.

The audience becomes fearful for Desdemona's fate. Dramatic irony is used here because the audience is well aware of Iago's wrath and hatred towards Othello. Brabantio warns Othello against trusting Desdemona and the senator tells Othello,

"Adieu, brave Moor, use Desdemona well."

This can be interpreted as an ominous warning, foreshadowing some disaster looming.

"My life upon her faith!"

Is ironical because now Othello is so trusting of Desdemona's faith yet later, he has a change of heart when he believes Iago's lies about her cheating, which has disastrous consequences.

Iago's self-confidence and manipulation with words is intriguing and frightening.

The act starts and closes in the same way with Roderigo and Iago conversing.

Once again, Iago is controlling the action. He speaks in prose when speaking with Roderigo. He seems to wholly trust Iago, he is unable to sleep, and threatened to drown himself because he lost Desdemona.

"I will incontinently drown myself."

Iago is exasperated at this ridiculous chatter and he scorns his love saying that he prefers to be a baboon than to be so fickle as to kill himself for some unrequited love.

"I would change my humanity with a baboon

Roderigo confesses his shame at being so much in love and being unable to control this overpowering love.

"I confess it is my shame to be so fond"

IAGO

Virtue? A fig! 'Tis in ourselves that we are thus or thus. Our bodies are our gardens, to the which our wills are gardeners. So that if we will plant nettles or sow lettuce, set hyssop and weed up thyme, supply it with one gender of herbs or distract it with many, either to have it sterile with idleness or manured with industry, why the power and corrigible authority of this lies in our wills. If the balance of our lives had not one scale of reason to poise another of sensuality, the blood and baseness of our natures would conduct us to most prepost'rous conclusions. But we have reason to cool our raging motions, our carnal stings, our unbitted lusts—whereof I take this that you call love to be a sect, or scion.

RODERIGO

It cannot be.

IAGO

It is merely a lust of the blood and a permission of the will. Come, be a man! Drown thyself? Drown cats and blind puppies. I have professed me thy friend, and I confess me knit to thy deserving with cables of perdurable toughness. I could never better stead thee than now. Put money in thy purse. Follow thou the wars; defeat thy favour with an usurped beard. I say, put money in thy purse. It cannot be that Desdemona should long continue her love to the Moor—put money in thy purse—nor he his to her. It was a violent commencement in her, and thou shalt see an answerable sequestration —put but money in thy purse. These Moors are changeable in their wills. Fill thy purse with money. The food that to him now is as luscious as locusts shall be to him shortly as bitter as coloquintida. She must change for youth. When she is sated with his body she will find the error of her choice. Therefore, put money in thy purse. If thou wilt needs damn thyself, do it a more delicate way than drowning. Make all the money thou canst. If sanctimony and a frail vow betwixt an erring barbarian and a supersubtle Venetian be not too hard for my wits and all the tribe of hell, thou shalt enjoy her. Therefore make money. A pox of drowning thyself! It is clean out of the way. Seek thou rather to be hanged in compassing thy joy than to be drowned and go without her.

Iago scorns his fickleness, and we can attribute his reasoning to a biblical imagery of the garden of Eden.

"Virtue? A fig!"

He refers to virtue as being a fig. After Adam and Eve ate the apple, they covered their nakedness with fig leaves. He further uses a metaphor,

"Our bodies are our gardens"

And our wills are gardeners. There is an imagery of reaping and sowing. If we sow weeds our garden will be barren and if we grow lettuce, productive. He associates this to our emotions and willpower which needs to be controlled and that we need to have rational minds to control our urges, so we do not end up in disaster like Adam and Eve. They disobeyed God and allowed their passions to control their reasoning which resulted in them being thrown out of the Garden of Eden.

Iago urges Roderigo to man up and he uses very compelling, flowery, persuasive language like a knitting imagery saying that he will knit a promise with strong cables to get Desdemona for him.

"I confess me knit to thy deserving
with cables of perdurable toughness."

Iago convinces Roderigo that the Moor's tempers will change, and that Desdemona will tire of his body and will go for someone younger.

Iago tells him to save his money and forget about drowning himself because he will get to sleep with Desdemona.

"and all the tribe of hell, thou shalt enjoy her

The use of religious reference where Iago is referring to 'hell' can be associated with his devilish thoughts and action. He can be associated to the devil because of his evil deeds.

RODERIGO
Wilt thou be fast to my hopes if I depend on the issue?

IAGO
Thou art sure of me. Go, make money. I have told thee often, and I retell thee again and again, I hate the Moor. My cause is hearted; thine hath no less reason. Let us be conjunctive in our revenge against him. If thou canst cuckold him, thou dost thyself a pleasure, me a sport. There are many events in the womb of time which will be delivered. Traverse, go, provide thy money. We will have more of this tomorrow. Adieu.

RODERIGO
Where shall we meet i' th' morning?

IAGO
At my lodging.

RODERIGO
I'll be with thee betimes.

IAGO
Go to, farewell. Do you hear, Roderigo?

RODERIGO
What say you?

IAGO
No more of drowning, do you hear?

RODERIGO
I am changed.

IAGO
Go to, farewell. Put money enough in your purse.

RODERIGO
I'll sell all my land.

RODERIGO ***exits***

EXPLANATION

Roderigo asks Iago if he will deliver on his promise.

Iago convinces him that he hates the Moor. He says that both their hearts have reason to hate the Moor and that both of them must be joined together in their revenge against him.

"Let us be conjunctive in our revenge against him"

The metaphor, 'womb of time' is important because the womb is associated with life and it's ironical that in a matter of time Desdemona will pay with her life.

IAGO

Thus do I ever make my fool my purse
For I mine own gained knowledge should profane
If I would time expend with such a snipe
But for my sport and profit. I hate the Moor,
And it is thought abroad that 'twixt my sheets
'Has done my office. I know not if 't be true,
But I, for mere suspicion in that kind,
Will do as if for surety. He holds me well.
The better shall my purpose work on him.
Cassio's a proper man. Let me see now:
To get his place and to plume up my will
In double knavery—How? how?—Let's see.
After some time, to abuse Othello's ear
That he is too familiar with his wife.
He hath a person and a smooth dispose
To be suspected, framed to make women false.
The Moor is of a free and open nature
That thinks men honest that but seem to be so,
And will as tenderly be led by th' nose as asses are.
I have 't. It is engendered! Hell and night
Must bring this monstrous birth to the world's light.

IAGO ***exits***

The play is dominated with the themes of deception and power. Iago dominates Roderigo, manipulates and lies to him.

Roderigo is so blinded by love that it supersedes his power of reasoning. Iago had already proved to be a selfish fraud, yet he can't see that.

"But for my sport and profit"

Iago clearly views Roderigo as a fool who he can extract money from. In his soliloquy he is mastering his skills of manipulation and he is concocting a plan to exact his revenge on Othello. He accuses the Moor of seducing his wife. His devious mind pounces on Cassio and he decides to usurp his position and use him to take revenge on Othello.

"To get his place and to plume up my will in double knavery"

He then decides,

"to abuse Othello's ear"

By tainting it with lies. He plans to take advantage of Othello's naivety saying that he will,

"as tenderly be led by th' nose as asses are"

Iago finally crafted out his plan.

"I have't" It is engendered! Hell and night
Must bring this monstrous birth to the world's light."

The use of the biblical imagery, 'Hell' associates Iago to the devil. Reference to 'birth' suggests that is plans will give birth to death and destruction.

ACT 2

SUMMARY

In scene 1

- There is a storm raging in Cyprus and it is reported that the Turkish fleet has been destroyed and everyone is worried about Othello's safety. Iago arrives with Desdemona ahead of Othello.
- Othello is secretly enraged about the love and cordiality that exists between Othello and Desdemona.
- He plans to destroy this love by accusing Desdemona of having an affair with Cassio.
- He asks Roderigo to provoke Cassio and incite some violence in him so that he can lose his job.
- Iago convinces Othello that Cassio is a drunk and that he was wholly responsible for the fracas.
- Othello is furious and he fires Cassio from his job for being drunk and disorderly.

In scene 2

- There is to be a party to celebrate the destruction of the Turkish fleet and Othello and Desdemona's marriage.
- Everyone will participate in the celebration and Othello demanded order.

In scene 3

- Cassio was given the task as overseer of the celebrations.
- Iago plies Cassio with huge amounts of alcohol, Roderigo antagonises Cassio, and a fight ensues.
- Cassio loses his job and Iago persuades him to seek Desdemona's assistance to be reinstated.
- He again promises Roderigo that he will win Desdemona over for him and he urges him to be patient.

TEXT ACT 2 scene 1

A Sea-Port in Cyprus

Enter
MONTANO *and two* Gentlemen

MONTANO
What from the cape can you discern at sea?
FIRST GENTLEMAN
Nothing at all. It is a high-wrought flood.
I cannot 'twixt the heaven and the main
Descry a sail.
MONTANO
Methinks the wind hath spoke aloud at land.
A fuller blast ne'er shook our battlements.
If it hath ruffianed so upon the sea,
What ribs of oak, when mountains melt on them,
Can hold the mortise? What shall we hear of this?
SECOND GENTLEMAN
A segregation of the Turkish fleet.
For do but stand upon the foaming shore,
The chidden billow seems to pelt the clouds,
The wind-shaked surge, with high and
Monstrous mane,
Seems to cast water on the burning bear
And quench the guards of th' ever-fixed pole.
I never did like molestation view
On the enchafed flood.
MONTANO
If that the Turkish fleet
Be not ensheltered and embayed, they are drowned
It is impossible to bear it out.

Enter
THIRD GENTLEMAN

THIRD GENTLEMAN
News, lads! Our wars are done.
The desperate tempest hath so banged the Turks
That their designment halts. A noble ship of Venice
Hath seen a grievous wrack and sufferance
On most part of their fleet.
MONTANO
How? Is this true?
THIRD GENTLEMAN
The ship is here put in,
A Veronesa. Michael Cassio,
Lieutenant to the warlike Moor Othello,
Is come on shore; the Moor himself at sea,
And is in full commission here for Cyprus.
MONTANO
I am glad on 't. 'Tis a worthy governor.

EXPLANATION

The scene moves from the organised social and political structure of Venice to that of the stormy, chaotic shores of Cyprus.

Shakespeare uses pathetic fallacy- the storm to reflect the raging passions and emotions of the characters for example Iago's sadistic nature and Othello's violent emotions.

There is also a sense of physical confusion where Othello is presumed lost in the storm and the Turkish fleet destroyed.

The use of the personification,

"Methinks the wind hath spoke aloud at land"

can suggest that the wind is warning us of the dangers that lay ahead.

Shakespeare uses a beautiful visual imagery here,

"The wind-shaked surge, with high and
Monstrous mane,
Seems to cast water on the burning bear."

The raging wind is compared to a fierce animal like the lion who represents Iago ready to pounce on the burning bear which can represent the passionate Othello.

News comes in that the desperate tempest had destroyed the Turkish fleet and the war is now over, but Shakespeare prepares us for a more boisterous war that is raging within Iago.

THIRD GENTLEMAN
But this same Cassio, though he speak of comfort
Touching the Turkish loss, yet he looks sadly
And prays the Moor be safe, for they were parted
With foul and violent tempest.

MONTANO
Pray heaven he be;
For I have served him, and the man commands
Like a full soldier. Let's to the seaside, ho!
As well to see the vessel that's come in
As to throw out our eyes for brave Othello,
Even till we make the main and th' aerial blue
An indistinct regard.

THIRD GENTLEMAN
Come, let's do so;
For every minute is expectancy
Of more arrivance.

***Enter* CASSIO**

CASSIO
Thanks, you the valiant of this warlike isle,
That so approve the Moor! O, let the heavens
Give him defense against the elements,
For I have lost him on a dangerous sea.

MONTANO
Is he well shipped?

CASSIO
His bark is stoutly timbered, and his pilot
Of very expert and approved allowance;
Therefore my hopes, not surfeited to death,
Stand in bold cure.

Voices cry within
A sail, a sail, a sail!

Enter
MESSENGER

CASSIO
What noise?

MESSENGER
The town is empty; on the brow o' th' sea
Stand ranks of people, and they cry "A sail!"

CASSIO
My hopes do shape him for the Governor.

A shot

SECOND GENTLEMAN
They do discharge their shot of courtesy.
Our friends, at least.

Cassio is worried about the Moors safety for they were,

"parted With foul and violent tempest"

Cassio arrives and it's the first time that we meet him. We know that he is bait for Iago, and we tend to get nervous for him.

Shakespeare deliberately portrays the Moor as being likable and a great commander,

"the man commands
Like a full soldier"

Ironically this description can be associated to the Moor's temper which is carefully hidden by Shakespeare for now because he wants us to witness Othello's downfall gradually.

Montana and the gentlemen go to search. for Othello,

"As to throw out our eyes for brave Othello"

There is a great contrast between Iago and Cassio. Whilst Cassio is polished in his mannerisms and speech Iago is course, and crude. Cassio is concerned about Othello's safety while Iago is nurturing his predatory nature to destroy Othello.

"O, let the heavens
Give him defense against the elements"

Cassio is very courteous and polite towards the ladies whereas Iago harbours misogynistic tendencies towards women. His attack on women during his verbal duel with Desdemona later in the play is evidence.

Cassio is disturbed about the noise, and he is told that everybody is down by the shore shouting,

"A sail, a sail, a sail!"

Cassio is anxious and he hopes that it is Othello being saved. The ship sounded out a friendly shot.

CASSIO
I pray you, sir, go forth,
And give us truth who 'tis that is arrived.
SECOND GENTLEMAN
I shall.
HE ***exits***

MONTANO
But, good lieutenant, is your general wived?
CASSIO
Most fortunately. He hath achieved a maid
That paragons description and wild fame,
One that excels the quirks of blazoning pens,
And in th' essential vesture of creation
Does tire the ingener.
Enter
SECOND GENTLEMAN
How now? Who has put in?
SECOND GENTLEMAN
'Tis one Iago, ancient to the General.
CASSIO
'Has had most favorable and happy speed!
Tempests themselves, high seas, and howling winds,
The guttered rocks and congregated sands
(Traitors ensteeped to clog the guiltless keel),
As having sense of beauty, do omit
Their mortal natures, letting go safely by
The divine Desdemona.
MONTANO
What is she?
CASSIO
She that I spake of, our great captain's captain,
Left in the conduct of the bold Iago,
Whose footing here anticipates our thoughts
A sennight's speed. Great Jove, Othello guard,
And swell his sail with thine own powerful breath,
That he may bless this bay with his tall ship,
Make love's quick pants in Desdemona's arms,
Give renewed fire to our extincted spirits,
And bring all Cyprus comfort!
***Enter* DESDEMONA, IAGO, RODERIGO, *and* EMILIA**
O, behold,
The riches of the ship is come on shore!
You men of Cyprus, let her have your knees.
HE ***kneels***
Hail to thee, lady, and the grace of heaven,
Before, behind thee, and on every hand
Enwheel thee round.
HE ***rises***

Cassio urges the gentleman to enquire who has arrived and to bring him word.

"I pray you, sir, go forth,
And give us truth who 'tis that is arrived."

Montano asks Cassio if his general is married. Cassio's answer is ironical because he paints a glowing picture of Desdemona. He says that she is beyond description- she is an ingenious person and is intellectually brilliant.

"One that excels the quirks of blazoning pens"

Iago arrives having weathered the storm,

"Tempests themselves, high seas, and howling winds."

One can connote that his sheer determination to get through the storm can be indicative of his determination to put his vile plans into action. Fate was on his side because the storm, just like Iago's boisterous character have helped him to arrive before Othello to carry out his sick plans. Cassio is already falling into his trap by showing his relief that Desdemona is safe,

"The divine Desdemona."

He also sadly refers to Iago as 'bold' unaware of his vile plans for him.

Will Othello bring Cyprus comfort with his stormy, fiery passions?

Once again Cassio is putting Desdemona on a pedestal and giving her Godlike status and bows to her.

"the grace of heaven."

He also refers to her as,

"The riches of the ship is come on shore!"

The exclamation suggesting his untold admiration for her. These innocent gestures of Cassio's are slowly digging his own grave.

DESDEMONA
I thank you, valiant Cassio.
What tidings can you tell of my lord?
CASSIO
He is not yet arrived, nor know I aught
But that he's well and will be shortly here.
DESDEMONA
O, but I fear—How lost you company?
CASSIO
The great contention of sea and skies
Parted our fellowship.
Within "A sail, a sail!" A shot.
But hark, a sail!
SECOND GENTLEMAN
They give their greeting to the citadel.
This likewise is a friend.
CASSIO
See for the news.
SECOND GENTLEMAN *exits.*
Good ancient, you are welcome. Welcome, mistress.
HE *kisses* EMILIA
Let it not gall your patience, good Iago,
That I extend my manners. 'Tis my breeding
That gives me this bold show of courtesy.
IAGO
Sir, would she give you so much of her lips
As of her tongue she oft bestows on me,
You would have enough.
DESDEMONA
Alas, she has no speech!
IAGO
In faith, too much.
I find it still when I have list to sleep.
Marry, before your Ladyship, I grant,
She puts her tongue a little in her heart
And chides with thinking.
EMILIA
You have little cause to say so.
IAGO
Come on, come on! You are pictures out of door,
bells in your parlors, wildcats in your kitchens,
saints in your injuries, devils being offended, players
in your huswifery, and huswives in your beds.
DESDEMONA
Oh, fie upon thee, slanderer.
IAGO
Nay, it is true, or else I am a Turk.
You rise to play, and go to bed to work.
EMILIA
You shall not write my praise.

Desdemona eagerly enquires about her husband's well-being.

"I thank you, valiant Cassio.
What tidings can you tell of my lord?"

It is ironical when Cassio says that the storm parted his and Othello's good fellowship because soon the despicable, concocted plans of Iago's will part their friendship.

Another ship has arrived, and it shot out a friendly greeting. Cassio asks for news. Once again, Cassio's love for Othello is displayed.

Shakespeare is preparing us for the terrible storm that Iago will create to destroy their love.

Shakespeare uses dramatic irony because we are aware of Cassio's fate, and now he kisses Emilia and apologises to Iago. Another nail in his coffin. Immediately Iago displays his appalling misogynistic and sexist behaviour with his war of words about woman. He slanders them profusely calling them noisy hypocrites and hussies,

"bells in your parlors, wildcats in your kitchen,
saints in your injuries, devils being offended."

Desdemona is shocked at Iago's clouded, cynical view of women and she too plays into Iago's hands by challenging him. She is unaware that this is Iago's ploy to discredit her.

TEXT ACT 2 scene 1

IAGO
No, let me not.

DESDEMONA
What wouldst write of me,
If thou shouldst praise me?

IAGO
O, gentle lady, do not put me to 't,
For I am nothing if not critical.

DESDEMONA
Come on, assay.—There's one gone to the harbour?

IAGO
Ay, madam.

DESDEMONA, *aside*
I am not merry, but I do beguile
The thing I am by seeming otherwise.—
Come, how wouldst thou praise me?

IAGO
I am about it, but indeed my invention comes
from my pate as birdlime does from frieze:
It plucks out brains and all. But my muse labours,
And thus she is delivered:
If she be fair and wise, fairness and wit,
The one's for use, the other useth it.

DESDEMONA
Well praised! How if she be black and witty?

IAGO
If she be black, and thereto have a wit,
She'll find a white that shall her blackness hit.

DESDEMONA
Worse and worse.

EMILIA
How if fair and foolish?

IAGO
She never yet was foolish that was fair,
For even her folly helped her to an heir.

DESDEMONA
These are old fond paradoxes to make
fools laugh i' th' alehouse. What miserable praise
hast thou for her that's foul and foolish?

IAGO
There's none so foul and foolish thereunto,
But does foul pranks which fair and wise ones do.

DESDEMONA
O heavy ignorance! Thou praisest the worst best.
But what praise couldst thou bestow on a deserving
woman indeed, one that in the authority of her merit
did justly put on the vouch of very malice itself?

EXPLANATION

She asks him what he would write about her, and he venomously answers that she must not tempt him because he foreshadows his plans and tells her that he will be critical of her,

"O, gentle lady, do not put me to 't,
For I am nothing if not critical."

Desdemona eggs Iago on to tell her what he thinks of her. It's as though she has some kind of premonition about him besmirching her character. Just like Cassio she too seems to be playing into Iago's hands.

Shakespeare uses dramatic irony because the audience is aware of the disgusting lies that Iago is concocting against her. She seems to be feeding Iago's predatory nature.

Desdemona is worried about Othello's safety, and this shows her genuine love for him. But she reverts back to her conversation to Iago about his opinion of her.

She says Iago's paradoxes about women is laughable.

"She never was yet foolish that was fair."

Iago's devious plot is slowly emerging from this conversation with Desdemona about women.

He says that if a woman is attractive, she will use her womanly wiles to get what she wants.

This is a subtle hint by Iago telling Desdemona that this very idea of seduction will be wrongly used against her later in the play which ultimately leads to her death.

These chilling ideas from Iago foreshadows how he is slowly weaving each strand of his web to ensnare these unsuspecting people which will eventually cause their demise.

Desdemona thinks that this conversation is all in jest, but she is unaware of the underlying deadly intent.

IAGO
She that was ever fair and never proud,
Had tongue at will and yet was never loud,
Never lacked gold and yet went never gay,
Fled from her wish, and yet said "Now I may,"
She that being angered, her revenge being nigh,
Bade her wrong stay and her displeasure fly,
She that in wisdom never was so frail
To change the cod's head for the salmon's tail,
She that could think and ne'er disclose her mind,
See suitors following and not look behind,
She was a wight, if ever such wight were—

DESDEMONA
To do what?

IAGO
To suckle fools and chronicle small beer.

DESDEMONA
O, most lame and impotent conclusion!
Do not learn of him, Emilia, though he be thy
husband .—How say you, Cassio?
Is he not a most profane and liberal counselor?

CASSIO
He speaks home, madam. You may relish him
more in the soldier than in the scholar.

HE *takes* DESDEMONA's *hand*

IAGO, *aside*
He takes her by the palm. Ay, well said, whisper.
With as little a web as this will I
Ensnare as great a fly as Cassio.
Ay, smile upon her, do. I will gyve thee
in thine own courtship. You say true, 'tis so indeed.
If such tricks as these strip you out of your
lieutenantry, it had been better you had not
kissed your three fingers so oft, which now again
you are most apt to play the sir in. Very good; well
kissed; an excellent courtesy! 'Tis so, indeed. Yet
again your fingers to your lips? Would they were
clyster pipes for your sake!

Trumpets within

The Moor. I know his trumpet.

CASSIO
'Tis truly so.

DESDEMONA
Let's meet him and receive him.

CASSIO
Lo, where he comes!

Iago very subtly makes cynical remarks about Desdemona's choice of husband in Othello. He is very slyly expressing his dislike of Othello in a very racist manner,

"See suitors following and not look behind"

She is shocked at Iago's rantings and turns her attention to Cassio and ironically asks him if he thinks Iago, is a terrible character.

"Is he not a most profane and liberal counselor."

Just like the raging storm Iago brings darkness into everyone's lives as seen in his asides.

Shakespeare presents us with a prey-predator imagery by using a web. Iago is the predator and hopes to,

"Ensnare as great a fly as Cassio"

Iago is using Cassio's gallantry to trap him,

"Ay smile upon her, do."

Iago says that Cassio's courteous advances towards the ladies can cost him his job.

Iago makes a crude joke about, 'clyster pipes'.

Enter
OTHELLO ***and Attendants***

OTHELLO
O, my fair warrior!
DESDEMONA
My dear Othello!
OTHELLO
It gives me wonder great as my content
To see you here before me. O my soul's joy!
If after every tempest come such calms,
May the winds blow till they have wakened death,
And let the labouring bark climb hills of seas
Olympus high, and duck again as low
As hell's from heaven! If it were now to die,
'Twere now to be most happy, for I fear
My soul hath her content so absolute
That not another comfort like to this
Succeeds in unknown fate.
DESDEMONA
The heavens forbid
But that our loves and comforts should increase
Even as our days do grow!
OTHELLO
Amen to that, sweet powers!
I cannot speak enough of this content.
It stops me here; it is too much of joy.
THEY ***kiss***
And this, and this, the greatest discords be
That e'er our hearts shall make!
IAGO*, aside*
O, you are well tuned now,
But I'll set down the pegs that make this music,
As honest as I am.
OTHELLO
Come. Let us to the castle.—
News, friends! Our wars are done. The Turks are drowned.
How does my old acquaintance of this isle?—
Honey, you shall be well desired in Cyprus.
I have found great love amongst them. O, my sweet,
I prattle out of fashion, and I dote
In mine own comforts.—I prithee, good Iago,
Go to the bay and disembark my coffers.
Bring thou the master to the citadel.
He is a good one, and his worthiness
Does challenge much respect.—Come, Desdemona.
Once more, well met at Cyprus.

All but **IAGO** ***and*** **RODERIGO** ***exit***

Othello and Desdemona finally meet, and it's obvious that there is overflowing love between them. Othello refers to Desdemona,

"O my soul's joy!"

Othello says that he hopes that after every tempest comes a calm referring to Desdemona as the calm.

Ominously Othello makes reference to 'death,' 'die' and he juxtaposes

"As hell's from heaven!"

All these elements will play a vital role in Iago's deadly plot against him.

Othello says that if he were to die, he will be happy, and his soul will be content because of Desdemona's love.

Othello also ominously makes reference to, 'unknown fate.'

And Desdemona says,

"The heavens forbid"

This can refer to the unknown destructive fate awaiting Othello and perhaps heaven forbade this union between these two.

Iago's snide aside remark that they are happy now, but he will ensure the destruction of that love. The theme of appearance versus reality surfaces once again when Iago says,

"As honest as I am."

Iago is anything but honest. He is only pretending to be honest. There is a jovial atmosphere albeit short lived because there is a danger lurking.

Othello is well-respected in Cyprus because of his social graces and military prowess, however we did not yet see the storm lurking behind his calm exterior.

IAGO, *to a departing Attendant*

Do thou meet me presently at the harbour.

(To Roderigo)

Come hither. If thou be'st valiant—as they say base men being in love have then a nobility in their natures more than is native to them—list me. The Lieutenant tonight watches on the court of guard. First, I must tell thee this: Desdemona is directly in love with him.

RODERIGO

With him? Why, 'tis not possible.

IAGO

Lay thy finger thus, and let thy soul be instructed. Mark me with what violence she first loved the Moor but for bragging and telling her fantastical lies. And will she love him still for prating? Let not thy discreet heart think it. Her eye must be fed. And what delight shall she have to look on the devil? When the blood is made dull with the act of sport, there should be, again to inflame it and to give satiety a fresh appetite, loveliness in favour, sympathy in years, manners, and beauties, all which the Moor is defective in. Now, for want of these required conveniences, her delicate tenderness will find itself abused, begin to heave the gorge, disrelish and abhor the Moor. Very nature will instruct her in it and compel her to some second choice. Now, sir, this granted—as it is a most pregnant and unforced position—who stands so eminent in the degree of this fortune as Cassio does? A knave very voluble, no further conscionable than in putting on the mere form of civil and humane seeming for the better compassing of his salt and most hidden loose affection. Why, none, why, none! A slipper and subtle knave, a finder-out of occasions, that has an eye can stamp and counterfeit advantages, though true advantage never present itself; a devilish knave! Besides, the knave is handsome, young, and hath all those requisites in him that folly and green minds look after. A pestilent complete knave, and the woman hath found him already.

Shakespeare very carefully crafted the character of Iago who, although we dislike his manipulative skills, we find him intriguing maybe because of his skills in creating ingenious concoctions for trouble. He orders Roderigo to meet him at the harbour and targets his weak spot by saying that men in love become automatically brave.

Iago is a master craftsman because he says that Cassio will be on guard, and he toys with Roderigo's emotions by telling him that Cassio is in love with Desdemona. He sets the cat among the pigeons and creates an instant rift between Cassio and Roderigo.

He says that she loved the Moor because of his fantastical lie.

"Her eye must be fed. And
what delight shall she have to look on the devil?"

Iago associates Othello to the devil who is evil and ugly. This constant racist demeaning reference to Othello shows Iago's intensifying hate towards him. He says that when the lovemaking gets boring,

"When the blood is made dull with the act of sport"

Iago assures Roderigo that Desdemona will look for someone more exciting and vibrant.

"nature will instruct her in it and compel her to some second choice"

Cassio is the perfect match for her because he's very gallant and he has a subtle eye for the women,

"devilish knave!"

He is young, handsome and everyone envies him.

"green minds look after"

RODERIGO

I cannot believe that in her. She's full of most blessed condition.

IAGO

Blessed fig's end! The wine she drinks is made of grapes. If she had been blessed, she would never have loved the Moor. Blessed pudding! Didst thou not see her paddle with the palm of his hand? Didst not mark that?

RODERIGO

Yes, that I did. But that was but courtesy.

IAGO

Lechery, by this hand! An index and obscure prologue to the history of lust and foul thoughts. They met so near with their lips that their breaths embraced together. Villainous thoughts, Roderigo! When these mutualities so marshal the way, hard at hand comes the master and main exercise, th' incorporate conclusion. Pish! But, sir, be you ruled by me. I have brought you from Venice. Watch you tonight. For the command, I'll lay 't upon you. Cassio knows you not. I'll not be far from you. Do you find some occasion to anger Cassio, either by speaking too loud, or tainting his discipline, or from what other course you please, which the time shall more favorably minister.

RODERIGO

Well.

IAGO

Sir, he's rash and very sudden in choler, and haply may strike at you. Provoke him that he may, for even out of that will I cause these of Cyprus to mutiny, whose qualification shall come into no true taste again but by the displanting of Cassio. So shall you have a shorter journey to your desires by the means I shall then have to prefer them, and the impediment most profitably removed, without the which there were no expectation of our prosperity.

RODERIGO

I will do this, if you can bring it to any opportunity.

IAGO

I warrant thee. Meet me by and by at the citadel. I must fetch his necessaries ashore. Farewell.

RODERIGO

Adieu.

HE ***exits***

Roderigo is shocked and Iago convinces him by attacking Desdemona's sexuality. He uses a biblical imagery,

"blessed fig's end!"

Referring to Adam and Eve's covering their nakedness with fig leaves after they had sinned. This foreshadows Iago's plan to use Desdemona's sexuality to destroy her.

He accuses her of, paddling her palm with Cassio's palm and develop,

"lust and foul thoughts"

For him. Iago urges Roderigo to anger Cassio by speaking too loudly or attacking his personality.

Iago manages to manipulate the unsuspecting Roderigo who is a pawn in Iago's deadly game.

Iago's devious tactics, and well-thought-out plans shocks the audience.

He says that Cassio is very short-tempered, and he is bound to strike. He encourages Roderigo to provoke him so that he can discredit him in Cyprus. He will get them so angry that he will be removed from his position. He promises that the only way for Roderigo to be happy is to have Cassio removed. He agrees to do it on one condition Iago promises to help him get Desdemona

IAGO

That Cassio loves her, I do well believe 't.
That she loves him, 'tis apt and of great credit.
The Moor, howbeit that I endure him not,
Is of a constant, loving, noble nature,
And I dare think he'll prove to Desdemona
A most dear husband. Now, I do love her too,
Not out of absolute lust (though peradventure
I stand accountant for as great a sin)
But partly led to diet my revenge
For that I do suspect the lusty Moor
Hath leapt into my seat—the thought whereof
Doth, like a poisonous mineral, gnaw my inwards,
And nothing can or shall content my soul
Till I am evened with him, wife for wife,
Or, failing so, yet that I put the Moor
At least into a jealousy so strong
That judgment cannot cure. Which thing to do,
If this poor trash of Venice, whom I trace
For his quick hunting, stand the putting on,
I'll have our Michael Cassio on the hip,
Abuse him to the Moor in the rank garb
(For I fear Cassio with my nightcap too),
Make the Moor thank me, love me, and reward me
For making him egregiously an ass
And practicing upon his peace and quiet
Even to madness. 'Tis here, but yet confused.
Knavery's plain face is never seen till used.

IAGO *exits*

This soliloquy is a deadly cocktail of Iago's sick imagination and his passionate desire for revenge.

His perverted and clouded judgement makes him believe that Cassio loves Desdemona and although he hates the Moor, he says that he will make a good husband to Desdemona.

He says that he loves Desdemona not out of lust, but she will fulfil his,

"diet my revenge"

Iago's conniving mind believes that Othello had an affair with his wife.

"the lusty Moor
Hath leapt into my seat"

He wows that he will take swift revenge because the thought is killing him,

"Doth, like a poisonous mineral, gnaw at my inwards"

He plans to make Othello so jealous with rage that all his powers of judgement will be clouded.

He hopes that the Venetian trash Roderigo be successful, and he will then poison Othello's mind,

"Abuse him to the Moor in the rank garb"

about Cassio and he will,

"thank me, love me, and reward me
For making him egregiously an ass"

He won't know that I'm making a fool of him with my deadly plans to destroy him.

A Public Place

Enter
Othello's* HERALD *with a proclamation

HERALD
It is Othello's pleasure, our noble and valiant general, that upon certain tidings now arrived, importing the mere perdition of the Turkish fleet, every man put himself into triumph: some to dance, some to make bonfires, each man to what sport and revels his addition leads him. For besides these beneficial news, it is the celebration of his nuptial. So much was his pleasure should be proclaimed. All offices are open, and there is full liberty of feasting from this present hour of five till the bell have told eleven. Heaven bless the isle of Cyprus and our noble general, Othello!

Othello's* HERALD *exits

Ironically, in this scene war and love is juxtaposed.

Othello is celebrating both his marriage and their triumph at war against the defeated Turks.

Note that there is a jovial, party atmosphere but this excitement will be short lived because there is a sense of evil lurking in the air, a devious scheme of destruction that Iago is plotting.

Othello is addressed as,

"our noble and valiant general"

But Iago will taint this nobility soon and the Herald asks Heaven to bless Othello,

"Heaven bless the isle of Cyprus and our noble general, Othello!"

TEXT ACT 2 scene 3

The Citadel

Enter
OTHELLO, DESDEMONA, CASSIO,
and Attendants

OTHELLO
Good Michael, look you to the guard tonight.
Let's teach ourselves that honourable stop
Not to outsport discretion.
CASSIO
Iago hath direction what to do,
But notwithstanding, with my personal eye
Will I look to 't.
OTHELLO
Iago is most honest.
Michael, goodnight. Tomorrow with your earliest
Let me have speech with you.
(To Desdemona)
Come, my dear love,
The purchase made, the fruits are to ensue;
That profit's yet to come 'tween me and you.—
Goodnight.

OTHELLO *and* DESDEMONA *exit,*
with Attendants

***Enter* IAGO**

CASSIO
Welcome, Iago. We must to the watch.
IAGO
Not this hour, lieutenant. 'Tis not yet ten o' th' clock. Our general cast us thus early for the love of his Desdemona—who let us not therefore blame; he hath not yet made wanton the night with her, and she is sport for Jove.
CASSIO
She's a most exquisite lady.
IAGO
And, I'll warrant her, full of game.
CASSIO
Indeed, she's a most fresh and delicate creature.
IAGO
What an eye she has! Methinks it sounds a parley to provocation.
CASSIO
An inviting eye, and yet methinks right modest.
IAGO
And when she speaks, is it not an alarum to love?
CASSIO
She is indeed perfection.

EXPLANATION

Othello's speech here foreshadows the events to follow. We must not allow the party to get too crazy.

"Not to outsport discretion."

Othello's naivety is surprising because he makes this absurd statement,

"Iago is most honest."

Iago is actually 'the devil's workshop' meticulously crafting out his downfall.

Othello tells Desdemona now that the wedding ceremony is over, it's time to consummate their marriage.

"The purchase made, the fruits are to ensue."

Iago with his manipulative skills moves the plot along, creates all the interesting actions, and he's also responsible for the tone and mood of the play hence getting the audience spellbound.

His crudeness about the sexuality of Othello and Desdemona is shocking,

"she is sport for Jove"

"full of game"

We can juxtapose Iago's crass response to Desdemona's sexuality – which he will use to destroy her, to that of Cassio's which is full of respect and admiration.

"She is indeed perfection."

IAGO

Well, happiness to their sheets! Come, lieutenant, I have a stoup of wine; and here without are a brace of Cyprus gallants that would fain have a measure to the health of black Othello.

CASSIO

Not tonight, good Iago. I have very poor and unhappy brains for drinking. I could well wish courtesy would invent some other custom of entertainment.

IAGO

O, they are our friends! But one cup;
I'll drink for you.

CASSIO

I have drunk but one cup tonight, and that was craftily qualified too, and behold what innovation it makes here. I am unfortunate in the infirmity and dare not task my weakness with any more.

IAGO

What, man! 'Tis a night of revels.
The gallants desire it.

CASSIO

Where are they?

IAGO

Here at the door. I pray you, call them in.

CASSIO

I'll do 't, but it dislikes me.

HE *exits*

IAGO

If I can fasten but one cup upon him
With that which he hath drunk tonight already,
He'll be as full of quarrel and offense
As my young mistress' dog. Now my sick fool
Roderigo,
Whom love hath turned almost the wrong side out,
To Desdemona hath tonight caroused
Potations pottle-deep; and he's to watch.
Three else of Cyprus, noble swelling spirits
That hold their honours in a wary distance,
The very elements of this warlike isle,
Have I tonight flustered with flowing cups;
And they watch too. Now, 'mongst this flock of
drunkards
Am I to put our Cassio in some action
That may offend the isle. But here they come.
If consequence do but approve my dream,
My boat sails freely both with wind and stream.

Iago's height of villainy is exposed here when he makes constant reference to Desdemona's sexuality.

This foreshadows his cruel intentions and his prejudices against women.

Iago uses his expert powers of persuasion to tempt Cassio to partake of wine although he refuses.

"dare not task my weakness with any more."

He hopes to make Cassio,

"full of quarrel and offense"

This is another step in his vicious, malignant scheme.

The audience is aghast at how meticulously Iago is weaving this web of lies and deceit and it's actually going unnoticed.

He seems to overpower everyone's thoughts and actions.

Shakespeare creates a lot of nail-biting suspense and tension. Iago is reintroducing war into this, 'warlike Isle' whilst celebrating peace, just as he is planning to introduce animosity and hate into Othello's marriage.

He has also set the scene for chaos and mayhem by making everyone drunk and he set the 'cat amongst the pigeons' by putting Cassio,

"in some action
That may offend the Isle"

Enter
CASSIO, MONTANO, ***and Gentlemen***
followed by
Servants with wine

CASSIO
Fore God, they have given me a rouse already.
MONTANO
Good faith, a little one; not past a pint,
As I am a soldier.
IAGO
Some wine, ho!
Sings. *And let me the cannikin clink, clink,*
And let me the cannikin clink.
A soldier's a man,
O, man's life's but a span,
Why, then, let a soldier drink.
Some wine, boys!
CASSIO
'Fore God, an excellent song.
IAGO
I learned it in England, where indeed they are
most potent in potting. Your Dane, your German,
and your swag-bellied Hollander—drink, ho!
Are nothing to your English.
CASSIO
Is your Englishman so exquisite in his drinking?
IAGO
Why, he drinks you, with facility, your Dane dead
drunk. He sweats not to overthrow your Almain
He gives your Hollander a vomit ere
the next pottle can be filled.
CASSIO
To the health of our general!
MONTANO
I am for it, lieutenant, and I'll do you justice.
IAGO
O sweet England!
Sings *King Stephen was and-a worthy peer,*
His breeches cost him but a crown;
He held them sixpence all too dear;
With that he called the tailor lown.
He was a wight of high renown,
And thou art but of low degree;
'Tis pride that pulls the country down,
Then take thy auld cloak about thee.
Some wine, ho!
CASSIO
'Fore God,
this is a more exquisite song than the other!
IAGO
Will you hear 't again?

Iago calls for more wine. He sings a jubilant song because his devious plans are now taking shape.

The repetition of the noun soldier has an ominous ring to it. He ironically sings that,

"O, man's life's but a span."

Cassio with his clouded judgement remarked,

" 'Fore God, an excellent song."

It's frustrating how gullible Cassio is.

It's symbolic when Iago compares the might of the English against the Danes, Germans and Dutch.

He symbolically represents the Strong English who can devour the Danes, Dutch and Germans and these can represent Cassio, Othello and Desdemona.

Iago is determined to destroy all of them because of hate and jealousy.

Iago embarks on another song expressing his excitement, while Cassio and Montana ironically drink to the health of their general. Iago talks about King Stephen, and he sings that,

"His breeches cost him but a crown"

One can connote that there is a bawdy sexual connotation as in keeping with Iago's vulgarity that the king lost his crown because of his promiscuity.

In the same way Desdemona and Othello lose their crowns – life and position, because of Iago's accusations.

TEXT ACT 2 scene 3

CASSIO
No, for I hold him to be unworthy of his place
that does those things. Well, God's above all,
and there be souls must be saved,
and there be souls must not be saved.

IAGO
It's true, good lieutenant.

CASSIO
For mine own part—no offense to the General,
nor any man of quality—I hope to be saved.

IAGO
And so do I too, lieutenant.

CASSIO
Ay, but, by your leave, not before me. The Lieutenant is to be saved before the Ancient. Let's have no more of this. Let's to our affairs. God forgive us our sins! Gentlemen, let's look to our business. Do not think, gentlemen, I am drunk. This is my ancient, this is my right hand, and this is my left. I am not drunk now. I can stand well enough, and I speak well enough.

GENTLEMEN
Excellent well.

CASSIO
Why, very well then.
You must not think then that I am drunk.

CASSIO ***exits***

MONTANO
To th' platform, masters. Come, let's set the watch.

GENTLEMEN ***exits***

IAGO, *to Montano*
You see this fellow that is gone before?
He's a soldier fit to stand by Caesar
And give direction; and do but see his vice.
'Tis to his virtue a just equinox,
The one as long as th' other. 'Tis pity of him.
I fear the trust Othello puts him in,
On some odd time of his infirmity,
Will shake this island.

MONTANO
But is he often thus?

IAGO
'Tis evermore the prologue to his sleep.
He'll watch the horologe a double set
If drink rock not his cradle.

MONTANO
It were well
The General were put in mind of it.
Perhaps he sees it not, or his good nature
Prizes the virtue that appears in Cassio
And looks not on his evils. Is not this true?

EXPLANATION

Cassio's use of biblical imagery is poignant. It foreshadows Othello's and Desdemona's fate where some will go to heaven and some to hell.

"and there be souls must be saved,
and there be souls must not be saved."

Cassio in his drunken stupor asks God to forgive our sins.

One can connote that it is an unconscious warning to Iago to heed the wrath of God for his unspeakable and sinful actions. Meanwhile Cassio is in denial insisting that he is not drunk.

Cassio exits, Iago seizes the opportunity to degrade Cassio.

"but see his vice"

We will look at Iago's conniving tactics, his masterpiece for success which intrigues the audience. He acts as though he is concerned and being nice yet, in fact he has a dagger in his heart. How can one person possess so much of evil we ask ourselves?

Iago takes the audience on an emotional journey. He fears that Othello holds Cassio in very high esteem and that he has a serious problem.

Iago lies that Cassio drinks himself to sleep,

"If drink rock not his cradle."

and he pretends that he wants to help him.

Montana innocently suggests that Othello needs to be made aware of this problem.

"Perhaps he sees it not"

***Enter* RODERIGO**

IAGO, *aside to Roderigo*
How now, Roderigo?
I pray you, after the Lieutenant, go.

RODERIGO *exits*

MONTANO
And 'tis great pity that the noble Moor
Should hazard such a place as his own second
With one of an engraffed infirmity.
It were an honest action to say so
To the Moor.
IAGO
Not I, for this fair island.
I do love Cassio well and would do much
To cure him of this evil—
"Help, help!" within.
But hark! What noise?

***Enter* CASSIO, *pursuing* RODERIGO**

CASSIO
Zounds, you rogue, you rascal!
MONTANO
What's the matter, lieutenant?
CASSIO
A knave teach me my duty?
I'll beat the knave into a twiggen bottle.
RODERIGO
Beat me?
CASSIO
Dost thou prate, rogue?

CASSIO *beats* RODERIGO

MONTANO
Nay, good lieutenant. I pray you, sir, hold your hand.
CASSIO
Let me go, sir, or I'll knock you o'er the mazard.
MONTANO
Come, come, you're drunk.
CASSIO
Drunk?

CASSIO *fight* RODERIGO

IAGO, *aside to Roderigo*
Away, I say! Go out and cry a mutiny.

Iago very craftily sends Roderigo to go after Cassio.

"I pray you, after the Lieutenant, go."

It's alarming at what speed and precision Iago can manipulative these men who do his bidding like stooges.

Montana says that it is a great pity that Othello should have Cassio as his lieutenant with such a huge drinking problem and insists that Othello be told.

"honest action to say so
To the Moor"

Iago's hypocritical response is shocking. He says that he loves Cassio very much and would never rat on him even if he was given the whole Island.

"I do love Cassio well and would do much
To cure him of this evil"

He is bent on helping him to cure this addiction.

Iago's plan had worked. Cassio is chasing Roderigo and he beats him.

"A knave teach me my duty?
I'll beat the knave into a twiggen bottle"

Montana urges Cassio to calm down and Cassio turns his fury on the unsuspecting Montana.

"Let me go, sir, or I'll knock you o'er the mazard."

Shakespeare adds a bit of humour here to cut the tension that is about to erupt. Iago belts out instructions to Roderigo to

"Go out and cry mutiny."

RODERIGO ***exits***

Nay, good lieutenant.—God's will, gentlemen!—
Help, ho! Lieutenant—sir—Montano—sir—
Help, masters!—Here's a goodly watch indeed!

A bell is rung

Who's that which rings the bell? Diablo, ho!
The town will rise. God's will, lieutenant, hold!
You will be shamed forever.

Enter
OTHELLO ***and Attendants***

OTHELLO
What is the matter here?

MONTANO
Zounds, I bleed still.
I am hurt to th' death. He dies!

HE ***attacks Cassio***

OTHELLO
Hold, for your lives!

IAGO
Hold, ho! Lieutenant—sir—Montano—gentlemen—
Have you forgot all sense of place and duty?
Hold! The General speaks to you. Hold, for shame.

OTHELLO
Why, how now, ho!
From whence ariseth this?
Are we turned Turks,
And to ourselves do that
Which heaven hath forbid the Ottomites?
For Christian shame, put by this barbarous brawl!
He that stirs next to carve for his own rage
Holds his soul light; he dies upon his motion.
Silence that dreadful bell. It frights the isle
From her propriety. What is the matter, masters?
Honest Iago, that looks dead with grieving,
Speak. Who began this? On thy love, I charge thee.

Roderigo goes out yelling and screaming and he rings the bell.

Iago says that the whole town will rise, and he pretends to subdue Cassio with much concern for him.

"The town will rise. God's will, lieutenant, hold!"

The raucous causes concern to Othello and Montana bleeds profusely from his wounds.

Othello is authoritative and takes command. The use of the exclamation suggests his mounting anger.

"Hold for your lives!"

Iago's vile pretences astounds the reader, and the hyphens can suggest his superficial concerns when he tries to cool them down.

The theme of appearance versus reality can be visible here.

"Hold, ho! Lieutenant - sir – Montano – gentleman –"

Othello is furious – note Shakespeare's repetitive use of various punctuations - ! ? denoting his rising fury.

Othello questions,

"From whence ariseth this?
"Are we turned Turks,
and to ourselves do that
Which heaven hath forbid the Ottomites?"

We see Othello's dark side because he threatens death to anyone who disturbs the peace.

"He dies upon his motion."

This foreshadows his later brutal actions when he kills his wife. It's ironical that Othello says,

"Silence that dreadful bell."

IAGO

I do not know. Friends all but now, even now,
In quarter and in terms like bride and groom
Divesting them for bed; and then but now,
As if some planet had unwitted men,
Swords out, and tilting one at other's breast,
In opposition bloody. I cannot speak
Any beginning to this peevish odds,
And would in action glorious I had lost
Those legs that brought me to a part of it!

OTHELLO

How comes it, Michael, you are thus forgot?

CASSIO

I pray you pardon me; I cannot speak.

OTHELLO

Worthy Montano, you were wont be civil.
The gravity and stillness of your youth
The world hath noted. And your name is great
In mouths of wisest censure. What's the matter
That you unlace your reputation thus,
And spend your rich opinion for the name
Of a night-brawler? Give me answer to it.

MONTANO

Worthy Othello, I am hurt to danger.
Your officer Iago can inform you,
While I spare speech,
which something now offends me,
Of all that I do know; nor know I aught
By me that's said or done amiss this night,
Unless self-charity be sometimes a vice,
And to defend ourselves it be a sin
When violence assails us.

OTHELLO

Now, by heaven,
My blood begins my safer guides to rule,
And passion, having my best judgment collied,
Assays to lead the way. Zounds, if I stir,
Or do but lift this arm, the best of you
Shall sink in my rebuke. Give me to know
How this foul rout began, who set it on;
And he that is approved in this offense,
Though he had twinned with me, both at a birth,
Shall lose me. What, in a town of war
Yet wild, the people's hearts brimful of fear,
To manage private and domestic quarrel,
In night, and on the court and guard of safety?
'Tis monstrous. Iago, who began 't?

MONTANO

If partially affined, or leagued in office,
Thou dost deliver more or less than truth,
Thou art no soldier.

The bell is symbolic of himself because he will be silenced after he kills Desdemona. Iago is so cool and calculated in his lies. His villainous nature surfaces again because he created this whole fiasco.

Iago vehemently denies any knowledge of the events, yet he was the architect of all this problem. He wormed his way out and orchestrated it by getting Cassio drunk who was a pawn in his deadly game.

By now Iago had created a sense of revulsion in the reader. He states that he preferred to lose his legs in battle than participate in this brawl.

Othello's speech to Montana is a reflection of himself, he tells Montana that he has a reputation for being civil and the whole world knows that. Wise people have the utmost respect for him but sadly Othello tells him,

"you unlace your reputation thus"

Montana still has faith on the wicked Iago and tells Othello that Iago will explain the events. Othello is losing his cool and he is becoming unhinged – demanding to know the details of this brawl and threatens them with physical violence,

"Shall sink in my rebuke."

Othello's violent nature is exposed for the first time. Shakespeare always portrayed him as a war hero and a respected gentleman. He even gives him the high social status of general.

Montana urges Iago to tell the truth and not to side with Cassio. If he does then he is not a true soldier.

Iago makes the audience despair because he is a devious agitator but the ease and the precision with which he manoeuvres his hideous and unpleasant deeds is indeed rather masterful and the audience can't help but be in awe of this enigmatic character.

IAGO

Touch me not so near.
I had rather have this tongue cut from my mouth
Than it should do offense to Michael Cassio.
Yet I persuade myself, to speak the truth
Shall nothing wrong him. Thus it is, general:
Montano and myself being in speech,
There comes a fellow crying out for help,
And Cassio following him with determined sword
To execute upon him. Sir, this gentleman

***Pointing to* MONTANO.**

Steps in to Cassio and entreats his pause.
Myself the crying fellow did pursue,
Lest by his clamour—as it so fell out—
The town might fall in fright. He, swift of foot,
Outran my purpose, and I returned the rather
For that I heard the clink and fall of swords
And Cassio high in oath, which till tonight
I ne'er might say before. When I came back—
For this was brief—I found them close together
At blow and thrust, even as again they were
When you yourself did part them.
More of this matter cannot I report.
But men are men; the best sometimes forget.
Though Cassio did some little wrong to him,
As men in rage strike those that wish them best,
Yet surely Cassio, I believe, received
From him that fled some strange indignity
Which patience could not pass.

OTHELLO

I know, Iago,
Thy honesty and love doth mince this matter,
Making it light to Cassio.—Cassio, I love thee,
But nevermore be officer of mine.

Enter* DESDEMONA *attended

Look if my gentle love be not raised up!
I'll make thee an example.

DESDEMONA

What is the matter, dear?

OTHELLO

All's well now, sweeting.
Come away to bed.
(To Montano)
Sir, for your hurts,
Myself will be your surgeon.—Lead him off.

It's all very well to detest such an obnoxious and abhorrent character like Iago but we should look at his sheer brilliance at how he single-handedly manipulated and fooled every character irrespective of social status. He said,

"I had rather have this tongue cut from my mouth"

This downright hypocrisy riles the audience at this cold, calculating liar. It was that very vile, vulgar tongue that had created all the pain and suffering.

He gives a detailed explanation of what happened and speaking with a silver tongue and choosing his language very carefully saying that he never heard Cassio swear before.

Gullible Othello praises Iago,

"Thy honesty and love doth mince this matter"

He thinks that Iago is defending Cassio.

When Othello sees Desdemona, he becomes even more irate. He threatens to make them an example.

This brawl with Desdemona now appearing, gives us a small taster of the bigger players to emerge later on.

Othello and Desdemona will take centre stage to fuel Iago's sick obsession of malice and hate.

TEXT ACT 2 scene 3

MONTANO ***is led off***

Iago, look with care about the town
And silence those whom this vile brawl distracted.—
Come, Desdemona. 'Tis the soldier's life
To have their balmy slumbers waked with strife.

All but* IAGO *and* CASSIO *exit

IAGO
What, are you hurt, lieutenant?

CASSIO
Ay, past all surgery.

IAGO
Marry, God forbid!

CASSIO
Reputation, reputation, reputation!
O, I have lost my reputation!
I have lost the immortal part of myself,
And what remains is bestial.
My reputation, Iago, my reputation!

IAGO
As I am an honest man, I thought you had received some bodily wound. There is more sense in that than in reputation. Reputation is an idle and most false imposition, oft got without merit and lost without deserving. You have lost no reputation at all, unless you repute yourself such a loser. What, man, there are ways to recover the General again! You are but now cast in his mood—a punishment more in policy than in malice, even so as one would beat his offenseless dog to affright an imperious lion. Sue to him again and he's yours.

CASSIO
I will rather sue to be despised than to deceive so good a commander with so slight, so drunken, and so indiscreet an officer. Drunk? And speak parrot? And squabble? Swagger? Swear? And discourse fustian with one's own shadow? O thou invisible spirit of wine, if thou hast no name to be known by, let us call thee devil!

IAGO
What was he that you followed with your sword?
What had he done to you?

CASSIO
I know not.

IAGO
Is 't possible?

EXPLANATION

Othello still puts Iago in charge to restore the peace and to,

"silence those whom this vile brawl
distracted"

Yet Othello will soon be the one silenced by Iago.

Iago's narcissism knows no bounds, he rubs salt on Cassio's open wounds. He asks him if he is hurting, and Cassio says that no amount of surgery can heal his wounds.

Cassio's lamentations about his reputation are very emotional, we tend to emphasize with him, his ruined reputation is in tatters.

Meanwhile Iago is revelling at his pain. He urges Cassio to go and plead his case with Othello, insisting that he still loves him.

Iago uses an imagery of the dog and a lion saying that he got to beat up the weak to set an example for the strong.

Cassio is disgusted with his terrible behaviour. His use of the repeated question marks suggests this.

"Drunk? And speak
parrot? And squabble? Swagger? Swear?"

He accuses wine of being the devil. Iago is pretending that he doesn't know the details of the fight and he quizzes Cassio.

CASSIO

I remember a mass of things, but nothing distinctly; a quarrel, but nothing wherefore. O God, that men should put an enemy in their mouths to steal away their brains! That we should with joy, pleasance, revel, and applause transform ourselves into beasts!

IAGO

Why, but you are now well enough. How came you thus recovered?

CASSIO

It hath pleased the devil drunkenness to give place to the devil wrath. One unperfectness shows me another, to make me frankly despise myself.

IAGO

Come, you are too severe a moraler. As the time, the place, and the condition of this country stands, I could heartily wish this had not so befallen. But since it is as it is, mend it for your own good.

CASSIO

I will ask him for my place again; he shall tell me I am a drunkard! Had I as many mouths as Hydra, such an answer would stop them all. To be now a sensible man, by and by a fool, and presently a beast! O, strange! Every inordinate cup is unblessed and the ingredient is a devil.

IAGO

Come, come, good wine is a good familiar creature, if it be well used. Exclaim no more against it. And, good lieutenant, I think you think I love you.

CASSIO

I have well approved it, sir.—I drunk!

IAGO

You or any man living may be drunk at a time, man. I'll tell you what you shall do. Our general's wife is now the general: I may say so in this respect, for that he hath devoted and given up himself to the contemplation, mark, and denotement of her parts and graces. Confess yourself freely to her. Importune her help to put you in your place again. She is of so free, so kind, so apt, so blessed a disposition she holds it a vice in her goodness not to do more than she is requested. This broken joint between you and her husband entreat her to splinter, and my fortunes against any lay worth naming, this crack of your love shall grow stronger than it was before.

Cassio is angry at his indiscretion, and he asks God why men are so stupid to indulge in something that will destroy their lives.

"O God, that men
should put an enemy in their mouths to steal
away their brains."

It is ironical that Cassio makes constant references to the devil whom he blames for his sorry situation,

"It hath pleased the devil drunkenness to give
place to the devil wrath."

Iago is certainly the devil here.

Cassio's drunkenness led to his anger. Iago pacifies him and insists that it would be wise to request his job back from Othello. Cassio is afraid that if he does that Othello will call him a drunkard.

The biblical imagery,

"Every inordinate cup is unblessed,
and the ingredient is a devil."

Can be attributed to the Last Supper when Jesus blessed the wine and gave it to his disciples.

We can associate Iago to the devil who gave his disciples unblessed wine to destroy them.

Iago pacifies Cassio and advises him to seek Desdemona's help to be reinstated in his job and he very crudely describes the relationship between Othello and Desdemona.

He eggs Cassio on to approach Desdemona to ask Othello for his job back.

"She is of so free, so kind, so apt"

And

"she holds it a vice in her goodness not to do
more than she is requested"

TEXT ACT 2 scene 3

CASSIO
You advise me well.
IAGO
I protest,
In the sincerity of love and honest kindness.
CASSIO
I think it freely; and betimes in the morning I will
beseech the virtuous Desdemona to undertake
for me. I am desperate of my fortunes
if they check me here.
IAGO
You are in the right. Good night, lieutenant.
I must to the watch.
CASSIO
Good night, honest Iago.

CASSIO ***exits***

IAGO
And what's he, then, that says I play the villain,
When this advice is free I give and honest,
Probal to thinking, and indeed the course
To win the Moor again? For 'tis most easy
Th' inclining Desdemona to subdue
In any honest suit. She's framed as fruitful
As the free elements. And then for her
To win the Moor—were 't to renounce his baptism,
All seals and symbols of redeemed sin—
His soul is so enfettered to her love
That she may make, unmake, do what she list,
Even as her appetite shall play the god
With his weak function. How am I then a villain
To counsel Cassio to this parallel course
Directly to his good? Divinity of hell!
When devils will the blackest sins put on,
They do suggest at first with heavenly shows,
As I do now. For whiles this honest fool
Plies Desdemona to repair his fortune,
And she for him pleads strongly to the Moor,
I'll pour this pestilence into his ear:
That she repeals him for her body's lust;
And by how much she strives to do him good,
She shall undo her credit with the Moor.
So will I turn her virtue into pitch,
And out of her own goodness make the net
That shall enmesh them all.

Enter **RODERIGO**

How now, Roderigo?

EXPLANATION

His misogynistic attitude surfaces once more suggesting that Desdemona is a loose woman. She will be able to patch up the rift between you'll.

Cassio is elated at Iago's suggestion, and he lies that he loves Cassio and that he has his best interests at heart.

Cassio agrees to meet with Desdemona and plead her case.

Note the juxtaposition in the manner Iago addresses Desdemona - full of vile expressions yet Cassio uses such dignified language, 'virtuous Desdemona'.

Cassio still addresses despicable Iago as 'honest'. Iago tries to convince himself that his sick actions are honest and good.

He's confident that he can win Desdemona over yet again making lewd references to her sexuality,

"She's framed as fruitful
As the free elements"

The Moor loves her very much, he will give up everything even his religion for her.

"His soul is so enfettered to her love."

He associates himself to the devil. He is trying to emulate the devil.

He says that when the devil wants to do something devious, he will put on his best appearance,

"When devils will the blackest sins put on,
They do suggest with heavenly shows
As I do now"

RODERIGO

I do follow here in the chase, not like a hound that hunts, but one that fills up the cry. My money is almost spent, I have been tonight exceedingly well cudgeled, and I think the issue will be I shall have so much experience for my pains, and so, with no money at all and a little more wit, return again to Venice.

IAGO

How poor are they that have not patience!
What wound did ever heal but by degrees?
Thou know'st we work by wit and not by witchcraft,
And wit depends on dilatory time.
Does 't not go well? Cassio hath beaten thee,
And thou, by that small hurt, hast cashiered Cassio.
Though other things grow fair against the sun,
Yet fruits that blossom first will first be ripe.
Content thyself awhile. By th' Mass, 'tis morning!
Pleasure and action make the hours seem short.
Retire thee; go where thou art billeted.
Away, I say! Thou shalt know more hereafter.
Nay, get thee gone.

RODERIGO ***exits***

Two things are to be done.
My wife must move for Cassio to her mistress.
I'll set her on.
Myself the while to draw the Moor apart
And bring him jump when he may Cassio find
Soliciting his wife. Ay, that's the way.
Dull not device by coldness and delay.

IAGO ***exits***

The theme of appearance versus reality can be seen here.

Iago is pretending to be virtuous but in reality, he is the 'devil in disguise'.

Iago plans to discredit Desdemona's virtue and poison Othello's mind by lying to him that Desdemona is lusting after Cassio."

Shakespeare adds some humour to ease the tension for the trauma that we are about to face. He also uses Roderigo's naivety and stupidity to give us a breather from all Iago's manipulation.

Roderigo still can't see Iago for the wretched villain that he is.

He lost his money and got a beating but chose to still be a slave to Iago.

"My money is almost spent, I have been tonight exceedingly well cudgeled"

Iago tells him that he is a poor man if he is impatient.

"How poor are they that have not patience!"

He once again falls prey to Iago's silver tongue and empty words.

Iago tells him that if he is patient, he will reap the benefits,

"Yet fruits that blossom first will first be ripe."

Iago makes his final plans and ruthlessly includes his unsuspecting wife in his vile scheme.

She has to make Desdemona favour Cassio and while Cassio is talking to Desdemona Iago deviously plans to take Othello to see the two together.

Iago has concocted this horrible but brilliant plan. His web of lies and deceit is almost fully woven.

ACT 3

SUMMARY

In scene 1

- Cassio was kind enough to pay and hire some musicians to celebrate Othello's and Desdemona's marriage, but Othello gets annoyed and pays a clown to dismiss the musicians.
- Iago says that he will take Othello away so that Cassio can speak to Desdemona alone. He has a vindictive motive.
- Emilia readily agrees to help, and she arranges the liaison between the two.

In scene 2

- Othello goes to inspect the fortifications in the town with Iago.

In scene 3

- Desdemona very kindly assures Cassio that she will do everything in her power to persuade her kind husband to reinstate him in his job. As soon as Othello arrives Cassio decides to leave, Iago notices this and tells Othello that Cassio is sneaking away and doesn't want to be noticed.
- Desdemona constantly badgers Othello to give Cassio his job back. He agrees to do so but her constant nagging on the subject, makes him start doubting her.
- Iago very craftily tells Othello that Desdemona is no longer interested in their marriage and has started looking elsewhere especially to Cassio.
- Desdemona mistakenly drops her handkerchief and Emilia finds it and she remembered that Iago asked her to steal it for him.
- She gives the handkerchief to Iago, and he taunts Othello about Desdemona's infidelity with Cassio which drives Othello insane with jealousy.
- Othello has murder on his mind. He wants to kill Cassio and Desdemona.
-

In scene 4

- Desdemona tells the clown to notify Cassio that she has put forward his case to Othello and pleaded with him to reinstate him.
- Othello asks Desdemona about the handkerchief, and he tells her that it is sentimental because it's an heirloom from his mum.
- He becomes very furious with Desdemona because she lost the handkerchief, and she lies to him that she didn't lose it.
- Emilia notices Othello's jealousy and she makes snide comments about men's temper and volatile behaviour.
- Bianca is furious with Cassio because he didn't come to visit her. She becomes angry when he gives her the handkerchief because she thinks that it is from another woman.

The Citadel
Outside Othello's Lodging

Enter
CASSIO *with Musicians*

CASSIO
Masters, play here, I will content your pains
Something that's brief; and bid
"Good morrow, general."

The Musicians play

Enter the Clown

CLOWN
Why masters, have your instruments been in
Naples, that they speak i' th' nose thus?

MUSICIAN
How, sir, how?

CLOWN
Are these, I pray you, wind instruments?

MUSICIAN
Ay, marry, are they, sir.

CLOWN
O, thereby hangs a tail.

MUSICIAN
Whereby hangs a tale, sir?

CLOWN
Marry, sir, by many a wind instrument that I
know. But, masters, here's money for you; and the
General so likes your music that he desires you, for
love's sake, to make no more noise with it.

MUSICIAN
Well, sir, we will not.

CLOWN
If you have any music that may not be heard, to
't again. But, as they say, to hear music the General
does not greatly care.

MUSICIAN
We have none such, sir.

CLOWN
Then put up your pipes in your bag, for I'll away.
Go, vanish into air, away!

Musicians exit

There's a change of scene here perhaps Cassio is trying to add some cheer to the tense situation which he had created.

He asks the musicians to play some music that will cheer Othello and he promises to pay them.

We see Othello's lack of sophistication because he doesn't like the music which is appreciated by the cultured and civilised minds of Venetian Society.

We further see his arrogance by sending the clown to dismiss the musicians. Hence Shakespeare prepares us for his downfall.

This scene helps to move the plot along and the action is rather continuous. The manner in which the clown attacked the musicians, and their music was very harsh.

"Then put up your pipes in your bag, for I'll away. Go, vanish into air, away!"

Cassio is falling so neatly into Iago's trap. Blind-sighted Cassio is trying to make amends for his terrible indiscretions, so he gives the clown money to arrange a meeting with Emilia.

TEXT ACT 3 scene 1

CASSIO
Dost thou hear, mine honest friend?
CLOWN
No, I hear not your honest friend. I hear you.
CASSIO
Prithee, keep up thy quillets.
Giving money
There's a poor piece of gold for thee. If the
gentlewoman that attends the General's wife be
stirring, tell her there's one Cassio entreats her a
little favour of speech. Wilt thou do this?

CLOWN
She is stirring, sir. If she will stir hither, I shall
seem to notify unto her.
CASSIO
Do, good my friend.

Clown exits

Enter Iago

In happy time, Iago.

IAGO
You have not been abed, then?
CASSIO
Why, no. The day had broke
Before we parted. I have made bold, Iago,
To send in to your wife. My suit to her
Is that she will to virtuous Desdemona
Procure me some access.
IAGO
I'll send her to you presently,
And I'll devise a mean to draw the Moor
Out of the way, that your converse and business
May be more free.
CASSIO
I humbly thank you for 't.

IAGO ***exits***

I never knew a Florentine more kind and honest.

EXPLANATION

Unbeknown to him that Iago is using his wife to assist him to weave his dark web.

Shakespeare is trying to show us that despite their social status men can be gullible and naïve. Iago enters centre stage as usual, and the audience is on tenterhooks about the outcome of his actions.

Iago controls the action of the play. He should, by now have acquired a sense of superiority because he so successfully managed to make puppets of all the superior people around him.

Cassio innocently relays to him that he had enlisted his wife to arrange a meeting with Desdemona.

Cassio again refers to Desdemona as, 'virtuous'

Iago speaks with a forked tongue acting as though he has Cassio's interests at heart, when he ensures Othello is out of the way, but in fact this was part of his devious plot.

Cassio in all his innocence is grateful for Iago's help,

"I never knew a Florentine more kind and honest."

***Enter* EMILIA**

EMILIA

Good morrow, good lieutenant. I am sorry
For your displeasure, but all will sure be well.
The General and his wife are talking of it,
And she speaks for you stoutly. The Moor replies
That he you hurt is of great fame in Cyprus
And great affinity, and that in wholesome wisdom
He might not but refuse you.
But he protests he loves you
And needs no other suitor but his likings
To take the safest occasion by the front
To bring you in again.

CASSIO

Yet I beseech you,
If you think fit, or that it may be done,
Give me advantage of some brief discourse
With Desdemona alone.

EMILIA

Pray you come in.
I will bestow you where you shall have time
To speak your bosom freely.

CASSIO

I am much bound to you.

THEY *exit*

Emilia becomes an unwitting accessory to Iago's deadly plot.

She kindly assures Cassio that everything will be fine, and that Othello and Desdemona are discussing your issues and she is speaking in your favour.

If you look carefully you will note that Iago has instilled in his wife his cunning style of speech.

She too makes negative remarks and follows it with positives for example, the Moor says that Cassio hurt someone very famous in Cyprus and because of that he won't reinstate you,

"That he you hurt is of great fame in Cyprus
And great affinity, and that in wholesome wisdom
He might not but refuse you

but he loves you and will try to reinstate you.

"But he protests he loves you"
"To bring you in again"

Note Emilia's contradictory manner of speech which mirrors Iago's.

TEXT ACT 3 scene 2

A Room in the Citadel

Enter
OTHELLO, IAGO, ***and Gentlemen***

OTHELLO
These letters give, Iago, to the pilot
And by him do my duties to the Senate.

OTHELLO ***gives*** **IAGO** ***some papers***

That done, I will be walking on the works.
Repair there to me.

IAGO
Well, my good lord, I'll do 't.

OTHELLO
This fortification, gentlemen, shall we see 't?

GENTLEMEN
We wait upon your Lordship.

THEY ***exit***

EXPLANATION

In this short scene the action and the pace of the events are moving at quite a rapid pace.

There's an ominous irony in this scene.

Othello is unaware of how his private life is slowing and meticulously falling prey to Iago's destructive artwork.

Othello is away on official business to check the fortification and Iago has arranged for Cassio to meet with Desdemona.

Othello gives some letters to Iago to give to the Senate. Iago appears very loyal and faithful calling Othello,

"Well, my good Lord, I'll do 't."

Before the Citadel

Enter
DESDEMONA, CASSIO, ***and*** **EMILIA**

DESDEMONA
Be thou assured, good Cassio, I will do
All my abilities in thy behalf.
EMILIA
Good madam, do. I warrant it grieves my husband
As if the cause were his.
DESDEMONA
O, that's an honest fellow! Do not doubt, Cassio,
But I will have my lord and you again
As friendly as you were.
CASSIO
Bounteous madam,
Whatever shall become of Michael Cassio,
He's never anything but your true servant.
DESDEMONA
I know 't. I thank you. You do love my lord;
You have known him long; and be you well assured
He shall in strangeness stand no farther off
Than in a politic distance.
CASSIO
Ay, but, lady,
That policy may either last so long,
Or feed upon such nice and waterish diet,
Or breed itself so out of circumstance,
That, I being absent and my place supplied,
My general will forget my love and service.
DESDEMONA
Do not doubt that. Before Emilia here,
I give thee warrant of thy place. Assure thee,
If I do vow a friendship, I'll perform it
To the last article. My lord shall never rest:
I'll watch him tame and talk him out of patience;
His bed shall seem a school, his board a shrift;
I'll intermingle everything he does
With Cassio's suit. Therefore be merry, Cassio,
For thy solicitor shall rather die
Than give thy cause away.

Enter **OTHELLO** ***and*** **IAGO**

EMILIA
Madam, here comes my lord.
CASSIO
Madam, I'll take my leave.
DESDEMONA
Why, stay, and hear me speak.
CASSIO
Madam, not now. I am very ill at ease,
Unfit for mine own purposes.

The dramatic tension is heightened in this scene.

The events are racing on at a fast pace to reach it's crescendo.

Desdemona very politely reassures Cassio that she will plead his case to Othello.

Emilia very innocently adds that Iago is very distraught about Cassio's situation.

Desdemona calls Iago, 'honest fellow!'

The exclamation suggesting her sincerity, yet she is sadly oblivious of the storm that is brewing around her private life, caused by Iago.

Cassio is very grateful, and he promises to be her faithful servant.

She assures him that it's just politics that's keeping them apart.

He said that he's afraid that the political considerations will drag on and Othello will forget his loyalty and love that they shared.

"My general will forget my love and service."

Desdemona adds

"My Lord shall never rest."

These are very poignant words because this is the start of Desdemona 'digging her grave'.

Shakespeare uses dramatic irony because Desdemona says,

"His bed shall seem a school."

Ironically, it is her marriage bed that will become a 'bone of contention' later in her demise. She says she,

"shall rather die
Than give thy cause away"

TEXT ACT 3 scene 3

DESDEMONA
Well, do your discretion.

CASSIO ***exits***

IAGO
Ha, I like not that.
OTHELLO
What dost thou say?
IAGO
Nothing, my lord; or if—I know not what.
OTHELLO
Was not that Cassio parted from my wife?
IAGO
Cassio, my lord? No, sure, I cannot think it
That he would steal away so guilty-like,
Seeing your coming.
OTHELLO
I do believe 'twas he.
DESDEMONA
How now, my lord?
I have been talking with a suitor here,
A man that languishes in your displeasure.
OTHELLO
Who is 't you mean?
DESDEMONA
Why, your lieutenant, Cassio. Good my lord,
If I have any grace or power to move you,
His present reconciliation take;
For if he be not one that truly loves you,
That errs in ignorance and not in cunning,
I have no judgment in an honest face.
I prithee call him back
OTHELLO
Went he hence now?
DESDEMONA
Yes, faith, so humbled
That he hath left part of his grief with me
To suffer with him. Good love, call him back.
OTHELLO
Not now, sweet Desdemona. Some other time.
DESDEMONA
But shall 't be shortly?
OTHELLO
The sooner, sweet, for you.
DESDEMONA
Shall 't be tonight at supper?
OTHELLO
No, not tonight.
DESDEMONA
Tomorrow dinner, then?

EXPLANATION

Shakespeare uses some unusual traits to develop Iago's sinister character to make him appear believable.

For example, his withdrawal of information, his hesitations, his silences and his pretending to have someone's interest at heart by first saying kind things about them and then laying on the dirt on them.

For example, he's never known Cassio to drink heavily.

Cassio leaves and Iago says,

"Ha. I like not that."

He planted a seed in Othello's mind then he pretends that he didn't see Cassio,

"Cassio, my lord? No, sure, I cannot think it
That he would steal away so guilty-like,
Seeing your coming."

Desdemona tells Othello that Cassio is grieving the loss of his job and your love. He made an honest mistake, and it wasn't done with malice.

"That errs in ignorance and not in cunning"

Desdemona's constant questioning was exactly what Iago wanted.

Note the continuous short, snappy line of questioning suggesting her desperation

"But shall 't be shortly?"
"Shall 't be tonight at supper?"

This gives Othello a sense of false belief that Desdemona is far too interested in pleasing Cassio. Iago is elated.

OTHELLO
I shall not dine at home;
I meet the captains at the citadel.
DESDEMONA
Why then tomorrow night, or Tuesday morn,
On Tuesday noon or night; on Wednesday morn.
I prithee name the time, but let it not
Exceed three days. In faith, he's penitent;
And yet his trespass, in our common reason—
Save that, they say, the wars must make example
Out of her best—is not almost a fault
T' incur a private check. When shall he come?
Tell me, Othello. I wonder in my soul
What you would ask me that I should deny,
Or stand so mamm'ring on? What? Michael Cassio,
That came a-wooing with you, and so many a time,
When I have spoke of you dispraisingly,
Hath ta'en your part—to have so much to do
To bring him in! By 'r Lady, I could do much—
OTHELLO
Prithee, no more. Let him come when he will;
I will deny thee nothing.
DESDEMONA
Why, this is not a boon!
'Tis as I should entreat you wear your gloves,
Or feed on nourishing dishes, or keep you warm,
Or sue to you to do a peculiar profit
To your own person. Nay, when I have a suit
Wherein I mean to touch your love indeed,
It shall be full of poise and difficult weight,
And fearful to be granted.
OTHELLO
I will deny thee nothing!
Whereon, I do beseech thee, grant me this,
To leave me but a little to myself.
DESDEMONA
Shall I deny you? No. Farewell, my lord.
OTHELLO
Farewell, my Desdemona. I'll come to thee straight.
DESDEMONA
Emilia, come.—Be as your fancies teach you.
Whate'er you be, I am obedient.

DESDEMONA *and* EMILIA *exit*

OTHELLO
Excellent wretch! Perdition catch my soul
But I do love thee! And when I love thee not,
Chaos is come again.
IAGO
My noble lord—

Desdemona is digging her grave deeper because her relentless goading will make Othello suspicious of her relationship with Cassio. She demands a date for Cassio to meet Othello.

"name the time, but let it not
Exceed three days"

I can't imagine you asking me something that I should deny.

She said that when she criticised him, Cassio would always defend him.

Othello is fed up with her constant nagging so he relents and says that he can come anytime he wants. Othello says that he will refuse her nothing. This shows his undying love for her.

There is an ominous irony developing. Desdemona seems to be antagonising Othello and causing a slight crack in their relationship.

He is now getting irate and requests for her to leave him alone,

"To leave me but a little to myself."

She says that she is obedient to him. Events are now taking a slow, dramatic turn.

It is ironical that Othello says,

"Perdition catch my soul"

Soon perdition will catch his soul when he kills Desdemona.

He will be experiencing eternal punishment and damnation for his deed. Iago is slowly creeping into Othello's mind and thoughts.

He is ready to put his final plans into action. He intends to play psychological games with Othello's mind. He asks if Cassio knew of the love between Othello and Desdemona.

TEXT ACT 3 scene 3

OTHELLO
What dost thou say, Iago?
IAGO
Did Michael Cassio,
When you wooed my lady,
Know of your love?
OTHELLO
He did, from first to last.
Why dost thou ask?
IAGO
But for a satisfaction of my thought,
No further harm.
OTHELLO
Why of thy thought, Iago?
IAGO
I did not think he had been acquainted with her.
OTHELLO
O yes, and went between us very oft.
IAGO
Indeed?
OTHELLO
Indeed? Ay, indeed! Discern'st thou aught in that?
Is he not honest?
IAGO
Honest, my lord?
OTHELLO
Honest—ay, honest.
IAGO
My lord, for aught I know.
OTHELLO
What dost thou think?
IAGO
Think, my lord?
OTHELLO
"Think, my lord?" By heaven, thou echo'st me
As if there were some monster in thy thought
Too hideous to be shown.
Thou dost mean something.
I heard thee say even now, thou lik'st not that,
When Cassio left my wife. What didst not like?
And when I told thee he was of my counsel
In my whole course of wooing, thou cried'st "Indeed?"
And didst contract and purse thy brow together
As if thou then hadst shut up in thy brain
Some horrible conceit. If thou dost love me,
Show me thy thought.
IAGO
My lord, you know I love you.

EXPLANATION

Shakespeare uses a lot of sensory imagery in this scene because everything depends on the senses like visual imagery, thinking, hearing and knowing. Later in Act 3 scene 3 line 387

"What sense had I of her stol'n hours of lust? I saw not, thought it not."

Othello has no proof of Desdemona's infidelity, but he has to depend on both his senses and Iago to find her guilty.

Othello asks Iago what he is thinking about and he says,

"As if there were some monster in thy thought Too hideous to be shown"

This dramatic irony is poignant because Iago's monstrous plot is too horrible to be shown.

Othello seemed to have picked up some of Iago's sinister moves, but he couldn't outwit his skill.

He noticed Iago's frowns, and the wrinkling up of his forehead as though he is imagining something terrible.

Othello suspects that Iago is withholding some information from him, and he urges him to reveal what he is thinking.

OTHELLO

I think thou dost;
And for I know thou 'rt full of love and honesty
And weigh'st thy words before thou giv'st them breath,
Therefore these stops of thine fright me the more.
For such things in a false, disloyal knave
Are tricks of custom; but in a man that's just,
They're close dilations, working from the heart,
That passion cannot rule.

IAGO

For Michael Cassio,
I dare be sworn I think that he is honest.

OTHELLO

I think so too.

IAGO

Men should be what they seem;
Or those that be not, would they might seem none!

OTHELLO

Certain, men should be what they seem.

IAGO

Why then, I think Cassio's an honest man.

OTHELLO

Nay, yet there's more in this.
I prithee speak to me as to thy thinkings,
As thou dost ruminate, and give thy worst of thoughts
The worst of words.

IAGO

Good my lord, pardon me.
Though I am bound to every act of duty,
I am not bound to that all slaves are free to.
Utter my thoughts?
Why, say they are vile and false—
As where's that palace whereinto foul things
Sometimes intrude not?
Who has that breast so pure
But some uncleanly apprehensions
Keep leets and law days and in sessions sit
With meditations lawful?

OTHELLO

Thou dost conspire against thy friend, Iago,
If thou but think'st him wronged and mak'st his ear
A stranger to thy thoughts.

Iago proclaims his love for Othello and Othello tells him,

"thou 'rt full of love and honesty"

Sadly, Iago uses reverse psychology by saying that he thinks Cassio is honest, yet he is bent on destroying him.

Ironically, Iago mentions the theme of appearance versus reality by saying that,

"Men should be what they seem"

Yet he's the one appearing to be good and noble but in fact is a scheming, wretched monster all out to destroy lives. Othello begs Iago to tell him his suspicions.

The pace of the play is moving so fast and the events moving so quickly that it is causing a sense of claustrophobia and tension amongst the audience.

Iago has got Othello in an 'iron grip' saying,

"I am bound to every act of duty"

Othello is vulnerable because at the beginning he says he doesn't know much about the world apart from fighting.

He finds conflict in his private life difficult to handle because he allows Desdemona the meeting with Cassio and asks to be left alone.

Furthermore, the racial barrier between them also makes him gullible to Iago's hateful revenge. Now Othello is deeply ensnared in Iago's trap.

IAGO
I do beseech you,
Though I perchance am vicious in my guess—
As, I confess, it is my nature's plague
To spy into abuses, and oft my jealousy
Shapes faults that are not—that your wisdom
From one that so imperfectly conceits
Would take no notice, nor build yourself a trouble
Out of his scattering and unsure observance.
It were not for your quiet nor your good,
Nor for my manhood, honesty, and wisdom,
To let you know my thoughts.

OTHELLO
What dost thou mean?

IAGO
Good name in man and woman, dear my lord,
Is the immediate jewel of their souls.
Who steals my purse steals trash.
'Tis something, nothing;
'Twas mine, 'tis his, and has been slave to thousands.
But he that filches from me my good name
Robs me of that which not enriches him
And makes me poor indeed.

OTHELLO
By heaven, I'll know thy thoughts.

IAGO
You cannot, if my heart were in your hand,
Nor shall not, whilst 'tis in my custody.

OTHELLO
Ha?

IAGO
O, beware, my lord, of jealousy!
It is the green-eyed monster which doth mock
The meat it feeds on. That cuckold lives in bliss
Who, certain of his fate, loves not his wronger;
But O, what damnèd minutes tells he o'er
Who dotes, yet doubts; suspects, yet strongly loves!

OTHELLO
O misery!

IAGO
Poor and content is rich, and rich enough;
But riches fineless is as poor as winter
To him that ever fears he shall be poor.
Good God, the souls of all my tribe defend
From jealous.

Iago actually tells Othello of his thoughts and actions which foreshadows his villainous behaviour,

"and oft my jealousy
Shapes faults that are not."

This is a deadly admission because he is falsely accusing Desdemona and Cassio of having an affair which will have serious consequences.

Iago tells Othello that it's important that people's reputation remains unblemished.

This ominous irony is disturbing because he targets Othello's reputation and he is adamant that he will not tell Othello his thoughts even,

"if my heart were in your hand"

Iago's brilliant choice of language is spine-chilling because he tells Othello that jealousy is

"the green-eyed monster which doth mock
The meat it feeds on"

And it is jealousy that Iago uses as a weapon to poison Othello's mind against Desdemona.
He says that a man is happy if his wife is cheating as long as he doesn't have to be friends with the man she's cheating with.

Someone who is poor and happy is rich enough but someone who is rich and is always afraid of being poor won't be happy. Iago is so hypocritical and calls on God to defend us from being jealous.

OTHELLO
Why, why is this?
Think'st thou I'd make a life of jealousy,
To follow still the changes of the moon
With fresh suspicions? No. To be once in doubt
Is once to be resolved. Exchange me for a goat
When I shall turn the business of my soul
To such exsufflicate and blown surmises,
Matching thy inference. 'Tis not to make me jealous
To say my wife is fair, feeds well, loves company,
Is free of speech, sings, plays, and dances well.
Where virtue is, these are more virtuous.
Nor from mine own weak merits will I draw
The smallest fear or doubt of her revolt,
For she had eyes, and chose me. No, Iago,
I'll see before I doubt; when I doubt, prove;
And on the proof, there is no more but this:
Away at once with love or jealousy.

IAGO
I am glad of this, for now I shall have reason
To show the love and duty that I bear you
With franker spirit. Therefore, as I am bound,
Receive it from me. I speak not yet of proof.
Look to your wife; observe her well with Cassio;
Wear your eyes thus, not jealous nor secure.
I would not have your free and noble nature,
Out of self-bounty, be abused. Look to 't.
I know our country disposition well.
In Venice they do let God see the pranks
They dare not show their husbands.
Their best conscience
Is not to leave 't undone, but keep 't unknown.

OTHELLO
Dost thou say so?

IAGO
She did deceive her father, marrying you,
And when she seemed to shake and fear your looks,
She loved them most.

OTHELLO
And so she did.

IAGO
Why, go to, then!
She that, so young, could give out such a seeming,
To seel her father's eyes up close as oak,
He thought 'twas witchcraft!
But I am much to blame.
I humbly do beseech you of your pardon
For too much loving you.

The repetition,

"why, why is this?"

Denotes Othello's dilemma. He will not live a life overwhelmed with suspicion and jealousy.

Othello uses the symbol of the moon which is a feminine symbol and it also symbolises death. Othello can unwittingly be referring to Desdemona's impending death.

He prefers to turn into a goat than become tormented and pained by the type of accusations that Iago is implying.

He is not going to allow the disparity in their social standing to hamper his love for her,

"Nor from my own weak merits draw"

He is confident that she chose him above all the other men.

"For she had eyes, and she chose me."

Note the use of visual imagery here and

"I'll see before I doubt"

He demands proof and that's when he will give up his love and jealousy, plaguing him.

Iago plants a seed of doubt in Othello. He tells him to observe Desdemona's reaction to Cassio and urges him not to be jealous or trusting.

"Wear your eyes thus, not jealous nor secure"

Iago's deviousness knows no bounds, he further torments Othello by pointing out that Desdemona deceived her father so she can deceive him.

Iago is trying to also usurp Desdemona's affection from Othello. He displays his false love towards Othello.

"For too much loving you."

OTHELLO
I am bound to thee forever.
IAGO
I see this hath a little dashed your spirits.
OTHELLO
Not a jot, not a jot.
IAGO
I' faith, I fear it has.
I hope you will consider what is spoke
Comes from my love. But I do see you're moved.
I am to pray you not to strain my speech
To grosser issues nor to larger reach
Than to suspicion.
OTHELLO
I will not.
IAGO
Should you do so, my lord,
My speech should fall into such vile success
As my thoughts aim not at.
Cassio's my worthy friend.
My lord, I see you're moved.
OTHELLO
No, not much moved.
I do not think but Desdemona's honest.
IAGO
Long live she so! And long live you to think so!
OTHELLO
And yet, how nature erring from itself—
IAGO
Ay, there's the point. As, to be bold with you,
Not to affect many proposèd matches
Of her own clime, complexion, and degree,
Whereto we see in all things nature tends—
Foh! One may smell in such a will most rank,
Foul disproportion, thoughts unnatural—
But pardon me—I do not in position
Distinctly speak of her, though I may fear
Her will, recoiling to her better judgment,
May fall to match you with her country forms
And happily repent.
OTHELLO
Farewell, farewell!
If more thou dost perceive, let me know more.
Set on thy wife to observe. Leave me, Iago.
IAGO, *beginning to exit*
My lord, I take my leave.
OTHELLO
Why did I marry? This honest creature doubtless
Sees and knows more, much more, than he unfolds.

Iago's words are like a double-edged sword, he is digging a grave for Othello, but he sugar-coats all his words. He so cruelly tells Othello that he knows what he said is hurting Othello,

"But I do see you're moved."

Yet he lies and says that it,

"Comes from my love."

He urges Othello not to take what he said too seriously.

Iago is revelling in Othello's pain. He twists the knife further into the wound when he says that Cassio's is his 'worthy friend' and again he insists that Othello is depressed.

Othello is adamant that Desdemona won't cheat on him and Iago's words have a dangerous, dramatic impact and foreshadows his deadly intentions —Desdemona's death.

"Long live she so! And long live you to think so!"

Iago very cruelly reminds Othello of his status, colour, and breeding. Iago's racial discrimination is seen once again,

"Of her own clime, complexion, and degree"

Saying that Desdemona turned down all these worthy suitors but now she harbours some dark and ugly desires.

In the Renaissance society men were very proud of their honour and a woman's reputation was scrutinised.

She had to be pure and chaste. That is why Iago targeted Desdemona's chastity and hence destroying Othello's reputation.

Now Othello is convinced of Desdemona's infidelity and asks Iago to observe her.

IAGO, *returning*
My lord, I would I might entreat your Honour
To scan this thing no farther. Leave it to time.
Although 'tis fit that Cassio have his place—
For sure he fills it up with great ability—
Yet, if you please to hold him off awhile,
You shall by that perceive him and his means.
Note if your lady strain his entertainment
With any strong or vehement importunity.
Much will be seen in that. In the meantime,
Let me be thought too busy in my fears—
As worthy cause I have to fear I am—
And hold her free, I do beseech your Honour.

OTHELLO
Fear not my government.

IAGO
I once more take my leave.

HE ***exits***

OTHELLO
This fellow's of exceeding honesty,
And knows all qualities with a learned spirit
Of human dealings. If I do prove her haggard,
Though that her jesses were my dear heartstrings,
I'd whistle her off and let her down the wind
To prey at fortune. Haply, for I am black
And have not those soft parts of conversation
That chamberers have, or for I am declined
Into the vale of years—yet that's not much—
She's gone, I am abused, and my relief
Must be to loathe her. O curse of marriage,
That we can call these delicate creatures ours
And not their appetites! I had rather be a toad
And live upon the vapor of a dungeon
Than keep a corner in the thing I love
For others' uses. Yet 'tis the plague of great ones;
Prerogatived are they less than the base.
'Tis destiny unshunnable, like death.
Even then this forked plague is fated to us
When we do quicken. Look where she comes.

Enter
DESDEMONA *and* EMILIA

If she be false, heaven mocks itself!
I'll not believe 't.

DESDEMONA
How now, my dear Othello?
Your dinner, and the generous islanders
By you invited, do attend your presence.

OTHELLO
I am to blame.

Notice the many hyphens at the end of Iago's speech, one can suggest that he is deliberately pausing for Othello to visualise all his vile and devious lies about his wife.

Iago's plan is coming into fruition and he is a destructive force, yet Othello cannot see beyond his façade.

Sadly, Othello trusts Iago fully,

"This fellow's of exceeding honesty"

He is prepared to let Desdemona go,

"I'd whistle her off and let her down the wind."

Othello's confidence is waning because he embodies and manifests Iago's negative view of Black men. He now questions the disparity in their social status, his physical appearance and his age,

"for I am black"
"for I am declined into the vale of years"

The hyphens in Othello's speech can suggest his fast-deteriorating mind and confusion.

He is fast and furiously sliding from celebrated war hero, of royal lineage, a romantic husband to tragic hero because of that great flaw in his character – overpowering jealousy. Othello mentions that

"forked plague is fated to us."

This forked tongue of a snake is a perfect description for Iago, who speaks with a forked tongue, plaguing Othello's life with his vile lies.

Othello uses a biblical imagery,

"If she is false, heaven mocks itself."

He accuses heaven of mockery, yet he is being mocked.

DESDEMONA
Why do you speak so faintly? Are you not well?
OTHELLO
I have a pain upon my forehead, here.
DESDEMONA
Faith, that's with watching. 'Twill away again.
Let me but bind it hard; within this hour
It will be well.
OTHELLO
Your napkin is too little.
Let it alone.
The handkerchief falls, unnoticed.
Come, I'll go in with you.
DESDEMONA
I am very sorry that you are not well.

OTHELLO *and* DESDEMONA *exit*

EMILIA, *picking up the handkerchief*
I am glad I have found this napkin.
This was her first remembrance from the Moor.
My wayward husband hath a hundred times
Wooed me to steal it. But she so loves the token
(For he conjured her she should ever keep it)
That she reserves it evermore about her
To kiss and talk to. I'll have the work ta'en out
And give 't Iago. What he will do with it
Heaven knows, not I.
I nothing but to please his fantasy.

***Enter* IAGO**

IAGO
How now? What do you here alone?
EMILIA
Do not you chide. I have a thing for you.
IAGO
You have a thing for me? It is a common thing—
EMILIA
Ha?
IAGO
To have a foolish wife.
EMILIA
O, is that all? What will you give me now
For that same handkerchief?
IAGO
What handkerchief?
EMILIA
What handkerchief?
Why, that the Moor first gave to Desdemona,
That which so often you did bid me steal.

Desdemona very lovingly and innocently offers to bind his painful head and he rudely declines her offer and in the interim the handkerchief falls unnoticed.

Emilia picks up the handkerchief which plays an important role in the play.

They were a means of communication between lovers in the Renaissance period.

The handkerchief was Othello's first gift of love to Desdemona and his rejection of it, and it falling can be symbolic of their falling marriage and Othello's rejection of her pure love.

Emilia innocently decides to give the handkerchief to Iago who asked her to steal it from Desdemona.

In the Elizabethan era women were very submissive to the males. They couldn't voice their opinion.

Note Iago's shabby treatment of his wife,

"To have a foolish wife."

And in Act 2 scene 1 line 114, Iago says,

"she gives you so much of her lips"

Emilia replies, line 123,

"You have no cause to say so"

Despite his demeaning of her, she is so keen on pleasing him,

"O, is that all? What will you give me now
For that same handkerchief?"

Iago's ruthlessness is shocking because he is prepared to use his wife in his sick game of hate and jealousy.

IAGO
Hast stol'n it from her?
EMILIA
No, faith, she let it drop by negligence,
And to th' advantage I, being here, took 't up.
Look, here 'tis.
IAGO
A good wench! Give it me.
EMILIA
What will you do with 't,
That you have been so earnest
To have me filch it?
IAGO, *snatching it*
Why, what is that to you?
EMILIA
If it be not for some purpose of import,
Give 't me again. Poor lady, she'll run mad
When she shall lack it.
IAGO
Be not acknown on 't.
I have use for it. Go, leave me.

EMILIA ***exits***

I will in Cassio's lodging lose this napkin
And let him find it. Trifles light as air
Are to the jealous confirmations strong
As proofs of holy writ. This may do something.
The Moor already changes with my poison;
Dangerous conceits are in their natures poisons,
Which at the first are scarce found to distaste,
But with a little act upon the blood
Burn like the mines of sulfur.

Enter **OTHELLO**

I did say so.
Look where he comes. Not poppy nor mandragora
Nor all the drowsy syrups of the world
Shall ever medicine thee to that sweet sleep
Which thou owedst yesterday.
OTHELLO
Ha, ha, false to me?
IAGO
Why, how now, general? No more of that!
OTHELLO
Avaunt! Begone! Thou hast set me on the rack.
I swear 'tis better to be much abused
Than but to know 't a little.
IAGO
How now, my lord?

She unwittingly becomes the main catalyst in Desdemona's destruction and demise because she gives the handkerchief to Iago which seals Desdemona's fate.

In all her innocence, Emilia asks Iago,

"What will you do with 't,
That you have been so earnest
To have me filch it?"

This is the turning point in the play and the plot is thickening because Othello demanded proof of Desdemona's betrayal.

Fate knocked on Iago's door yet again because he attained the handkerchief and put it into Cassio's room.

Othello's mind is poisoned with Iago's deadly lies about Desdemona's affair with Cassio.

"The Moor already changes with my poison."

Othello enters and Iago is ready to pounce on him. No number of drugs, or syrups, would have given him the sleep he had yesterday, Iago says.

Othello is angry with Iago for torturing his mind.

"Avaunt! Begone! Thou has set me on the rack."

The repeated exclamation mark can suggest his mounting anger.

The rack was a torture instrument in Medieval times where the arms and legs were stretched.

It's imperative that we look at the structure, tone, mood and pace of this scene.

We will also look at entrances and exits. There are also a lot of mirroring in this scene for example, Iago's choice of victims, in Act 2, he caused chaos in Roderigo's life and now he is doing the same thing to Othello.

OTHELLO
What sense had I of her stol'n hours of lust?
I saw 't not, thought it not; it harmed not me.
I slept the next night well, fed well,
was free and merry.
I found not Cassio's kisses on her lips.
He that is robbed, not wanting what is stol'n,
Let him not know 't, and he's not robbed at all.

IAGO
I am sorry to hear this.

OTHELLO
I had been happy if the general camp,
Pioners and all, had tasted her sweet body,
So I had nothing known. O, now, forever
Farewell the tranquil mind! Farewell content!
Farewell the plumed troops and the big wars
That makes ambition virtue! O, farewell!
Farewell the neighing steed and the shrill trump,
The spirit-stirring drum, th' ear-piercing fife,
The royal banner, and all quality,
Pride, pomp, and circumstance of glorious war!
And O you mortal engines, whose rude throats
Th' immortal Jove's dread clamours counterfeit,
Farewell! Othello's occupation's gone!

IAGO
Is 't possible, my lord?

OTHELLO
Villain, be sure thou prove my love a whore!
Be sure of it. Give me the ocular proof,
Or, by the worth of mine eternal soul,
Thou hadst been better have been born a dog
Than answer my waked wrath.

IAGO
Is 't come to this?

OTHELLO
Make me to see 't, or at the least so prove it
That the probation bear no hinge nor loop
To hang a doubt on, or woe upon thy life!

IAGO
My noble lord—

OTHELLO
If thou dost slander her and torture me,
Never pray more. Abandon all remorse;
On horror's head horrors accumulate;
Do deeds to make heaven weep, all Earth amazed;
For nothing canst thou to damnation add
Greater than that.

To Roderigo - a physical damage and Othello - a mental and psychological one.

Iago 'rules the roost' with both his cunning and his piousness.

His victims simply cannot escape him. He conducts most of the actions and the dialogue. He also adopts different tones – sometimes gay and sometimes pessimistic and hypocritical. He also depresses his victims, hence creating a melancholy mood.

Iago dominates the stage with his ever-present entrances.

Othello is a broken man, and he bids farewell to his life as a soldier and to his happiness.

"Farewell! Othello's occupation's gone!"

The repeated exclamation marks can suggest an ominous finality as though he is preparing to do something deadly and dangerous.

Othello threatens Iago with death if he doesn't prove Desdemona's infidelity.

"Villain, be sure thou prove my love a whore! Be sure of it. Give me the ocular proof."

He uses the sensory imagery of sight. Sadly, he wants Iago to be his eyes.

Iago is very expressive when he insists that he is honestly helping a friend.

IAGO
O grace! O heaven forgive me!
Are you a man? Have you a soul or sense?
God b' wi' you. Take mine office.—O wretched fool,
That liv'st to make thine honesty a vice!—
O monstrous world! Take note, take note, O world:
To be direct and honest is not safe.—
I thank you for this profit, and from hence
I'll love no friend, sith love breeds such offense.

OTHELLO
Nay, stay. Thou shouldst be honest.

IAGO
I should be wise; for honesty's a fool
And loses that it works for.

OTHELLO
By the world,
I think my wife be honest and think she is not.
I think that thou art just and think thou art not.
I'll have some proof! Her name, that was as fresh
As Dian's visage, is now begrimed and black
As mine own face. If there be cords, or knives,
Poison, or fire, or suffocating streams,
I'll not endure it. Would I were satisfied!

IAGO
I see you are eaten up with passion.
I do repent me that I put it to you.
You would be satisfied?

OTHELLO
Would? Nay, and I will.

IAGO
And may; but how? How satisfied, my lord?
Would you, the supervisor, grossly gape on,
Behold her topped?

OTHELLO
Death and damnation! O!

IAGO
It were a tedious difficulty, I think,
To bring them to that prospect. Damn them then
If ever mortal eyes do see them bolster
More than their own! What then? How then?
What shall I say? Where's satisfaction?
It is impossible you should see this,
Were they as prime as goats, as hot as monkeys,
As salt as wolves in pride, and fools as gross
As ignorance made drunk. But yet I say,
If imputation and strong circumstances
Which lead directly to the door of truth
Will give you satisfaction, you might have 't.

OTHELLO
Give me a living reason she's disloyal.

He threatens to give up his position,

"O wretched fool,
That livest to make thine honesty a vice!"

But Othello weakens and asks him to stay,

"Nay, stay. Thou shouldst be honest."

It's ironical that the adjective honest is used often.

"I should be wise for honesty's a fool."

Yet it is this false honesty which is the root of all the evil that ultimately causes Othello's downfall.

Othello is confused with juxtaposing thoughts of Desdemona's infidelity - thinking that she is honest and then thinking that she is not.

He associates her with Diana, the goddess of chastity and purity but now her name is,

"begrimed and black
As mine own face."

His sense of inferiority because of his colour is evident here.

Ironically, he associates Desdemona's defiled name as, 'begrimed' and 'black'. Othello is grappling with his sanity, he thinks about deadly weapons, 'knives', 'poison' or 'fire' leading us to believe that he is on a deadly mission.

Iago pretends that he is sorry for putting Othello in this misery. He uses some crude graphic imagery of Desdemona's and Cassio's union,

"Would you, the supervisor, grossly gape on, Behold her topped?"

Note Iago's speech is riddled with many rhetorical questions which he uses as a power of persuasion. This gets Othello thinking, answering and visualising the sordid scenario between his wife and Cassio.

IAGO
I do not like the office,
But sith I am entered in this cause so far,
Pricked to 't by foolish honesty and love,
I will go on. I lay with Cassio lately,
And being troubled with a raging tooth
I could not sleep. There are a kind of men
So loose of soul that in their sleeps will mutter
Their affairs. One of this kind is Cassio.
In sleep I heard him say "Sweet Desdemona,
Let us be wary, let us hide our loves."
And then, sir, would he gripe and wring my hand,
Cry "O sweet creature!" then kiss me hard,
As if he plucked up kisses by the roots
That grew upon my lips; then laid his leg
O'er my thigh, and sighed, and kissed, and then
Cried "Cursèd fate that gave thee to the Moor!"

OTHELLO
O monstrous! Monstrous!

IAGO
Nay, this was but his dream.

OTHELLO
But this denoted a foregone conclusion.
'Tis a shrewd doubt, though it be but a dream.

IAGO
And this may help to thicken other proofs
That do demonstrate thinly.

OTHELLO
I'll tear her all to pieces.

IAGO
Nay, but be wise. Yet we see nothing done.
She may be honest yet. Tell me but this:
Have you not sometimes seen a handkerchief
Spotted with strawberries in your wife's hand?

OTHELLO
I gave her such a one. 'Twas my first gift.

IAGO
I know not that, but such a handkerchief—
I am sure it was your wife's—did I today
See Cassio wipe his beard with.

OTHELLO
If it be that—

IAGO
If it be that, or any that was hers,
It speaks against her with the other proofs.

Iago asks Othello if he wants circumstantial evidence, so he concocted a bizarre but believable dream of how he lay next to Cassio and he heard him say,

"Sweet Desdemona,
Let us be wary, let us hide our loves."

And then Cassio grabbed his hand and cried,

"O sweet creature!"

And he kissed him so hard on the lips and then he laid his leg over his thigh and kissed him and said,

"Cursed fate that gave thee to the Moor!"

This graphic lewd dream drove Othello crazy, and he yelled in pain,

"O monstrous! Monstrous!"

The repeated exclamation mark shows his pain.

Iago has now managed to break Othello's spirit. Othello's thoughts and manner of speech is fractured and disjointed.

The onomatopoeia,

"I'll tear her to pieces."

Suggests this. Iago goads him on by using short, snappy sentences which increases the pace and the urgency of his intentions.

"Nay, but be wise. Yet we see nothing done."

It also highlights Iago's excitement at how meticulously his plans are working out. Iago wants the action to move on swiftly so that his plans are not marred. He quickly unravelled the false tale about the handkerchief to Othello.

"But such a handkerchief –
I am sure it was your wife's – did I today
See Cassio wipe his beard with."

TEXT ACT 3 scene 3

OTHELLO
O, that the slave had forty thousand lives!
One is too poor, too weak for my revenge.
Now do I see 'tis true. Look here, Iago,
All my fond love thus do I blow to heaven.
'Tis gone.
Arise, black vengeance, from the hollow hell!
Yield up, O love, thy crown and hearted throne
To tyrannous hate! Swell, bosom, with thy fraught,
For 'tis of aspics' tongues!

IAGO
Yet be content.

OTHELLO
O, blood, blood, blood!

IAGO
Patience, I say. Your mind perhaps may change.

OTHELLO
Never, Iago. Like to the Pontic Sea,
Whose icy current and compulsive course
Ne'er feels retiring ebb, but keeps due on
To the Propontic and the Hellespont,
Even so my bloody thoughts, with violent pace
Shall ne'er look back, ne'er ebb to humble love,
Till that a capable and wide revenge
Swallow them up.

HE *kneels*
Now by yond marble heaven
In the due reverence of a sacred vow,
I here engage my words.

HE *kneels*

IAGO
Do not rise yet.
Witness, you ever-burning lights above,
You elements that clip us round about,
Witness that here Iago doth give up
The execution of his wit, hands, heart
To wronged Othello's service! Let him command,
And to obey shall be in me remorse,
What bloody business ever.

THEY *rise*

OTHELLO
I greet thy love
Not with vain thanks
But with acceptance bounteous,
And will upon the instant put thee to 't.
Within these three days let me hear thee say
That Cassio's not alive.

IAGO
My friend is dead.
'Tis done at your request. But let her live.

EXPLANATION

The hyphens suggesting Iago's pretended hesitation to reveal his plans. Othello's speech is threatening when he talks about his vicious revenge on Cassio.

"too weak for my revenge"

He juxtaposes this by using dark imagery and visions of hell,

"Arise, black vengeance, from the hollow hell!"

This reflects his dark, vicious thoughts and the damnation of his soul.

"To tyrannous hate!"

We see an outpouring of his grief and revulsion, and he expresses this using an imagery of snakes' tongues.

"For 'tis of aspics' tongues!"

The snakes' tongues can be associated with Iago's deadly forked tongue, full of terrible lies. Othello screams,

"O blood, blood, blood!"

These words show us Othello's resolve.

He also uses a biblical imagery, 'heaven' and one can connote that his proposed actions are against heaven and God.

TEXT ACT 3 scene 3

OTHELLO

Damn her, lewd minx! O, damn her, damn her!
Come, go with me apart. I will withdraw
To furnish me with some swift means of death
For the fair devil. Now art thou my lieutenant.

IAGO

I am your own forever.

THEY ***exit***

EXPLANATION

This foreshadows his actions later on when he kills Desdemona. Othello shows his fury towards Desdemona,

"Damn her, lewd minx! O, damn her, damn her!"

Iago then surrenders his services to Othello no matter how bloody.

"I am your own forever."

He is ready to destroy Othello.

Before the Citadel

Enter
DESDEMONA, ***EMILIA, and*** **CLOWN**

DESDEMONA
Do you know, sirrah,
Where Lieutenant Cassio lies?
CLOWN
I dare not say he lies anywhere.
DESDEMONA
Why, man?
CLOWN
He's a soldier, and for me to say a soldier lies,
'tis stabbing.
DESDEMONA
Go to! Where lodges he?
CLOWN
To tell you where he lodges is to tell you where I lie.
DESDEMONA
Can anything be made of this?
CLOWN
I know not where he lodges; and for me to
devise a lodging and say he lies here, or he lies
there, were to lie in mine own throat.
DESDEMONA
Can you inquire him out, and be edified by report?
CLOWN
I will catechize the world for him—
that is, make questions, and by them answer.
DESDEMONA
Seek him, bid him come hither.
Tell him I have moved my lord on his behalf
And hope all will be well.
CLOWN
To do this is within the compass of man's wit,
And therefore I will attempt the doing it.

CLOWN ***exits***

Desdemona is enquiring about Cassio,

"Where Lieutenant Cassio lies?"

There is a pun on the verb 'lies', and the clown plays along with words.

This is symbolic because it is Iago's play on words that will cause Desdemona's ultimate destruction. She is persistent in her quest to find Cassio. You will notice that all the women Desdemona, Emilia and even Bianca are ruled by the men.

Desdemona is trying to interfere with her husband's state business in persuading Othello to reinstate Cassio, but she is looked upon with disdain.

The fact that she is a woman encourages Iago to find it very easy to make her his prime victim.

Iago treats Emilia very shabbily but despite that she steals and lies for him.

Bianca is also neglected and pushed aside by Cassio.

Women in the male-dominated Venetian society were under the jurisdiction of men and were treated as second class citizens with no voice or opinions of their own.

They were seen as commodities that were owned by men, just as Brabantio felt that Desdemona was his property.

TEXT ACT 3 scene 4

DESDEMONA
Where should I lose that handkerchief, Emilia?
EMILIA
I know not, madam.
DESDEMONA
Believe me, I had rather have lost my purse
Full of crusadoes. And but my noble Moor
Is true of mind and made of no such baseness
As jealous creatures are, it were enough
To put him to ill thinking.
EMILIA
Is he not jealous?
DESDEMONA
Who, he? I think the sun where he was born
Drew all such humours from him.
EMILIA
Look where he comes.

***Enter* OTHELLO**

DESDEMONA
I will not leave him now till Cassio
Be called to him.—How is 't with you, my lord?
OTHELLO
Well, my good lady.
Aside
O, hardness to dissemble!
How do you, Desdemona?
DESDEMONA
Well, my good lord.
OTHELLO
Give me your hand. *He takes her hand.*
This hand is moist, my lady.
DESDEMONA
It yet has felt no age nor known no sorrow.
OTHELLO
This argues fruitfulness and liberal heart.
Hot, hot, and moist. This hand of yours requires
A sequester from liberty, fasting and prayer,
Much castigation, exercise devout;
For here's a young and sweating devil here
That commonly rebels.
'Tis a good hand, a frank one.
DESDEMONA
You may indeed say so,
For 'twas that hand that gave away my heart.
OTHELLO
A liberal hand! The hearts of old gave hands,
But our new heraldry is hands, not hearts.
DESDEMONA
I cannot speak of this. Come now, your promise.

EXPLANATION

Desdemona is looking for her handkerchief because it's of much sentimental value and a symbol of Othello's love.

Shakespeare uses dramatic irony because the audience is well aware of the handkerchief in Iago's possession.

She unwittingly foreshadows the Moor's jealousy,

"made of no such baseness
As jealous creatures are"

But, in reality, his jealousy is brewing.

Desdemona's persistence for Othello to reinstate Cassio is inching her closer to her death. Othello takes her hand and comments that it is moist, and she replies it's that way because it had felt no sadness. Ironically, it will soon feel sorrow.

Desdemona is unaware that Othello is being sarcastic and crude with the comments about her hands.

"Hot, hot, and moist"

He implies that she gives her hand away freely to Cassio to have physical contact with him.

She needs to fast and pray so that she will not be tempted to look at other men. She is still innocent of Othello's accusations and tells him that it was her hand that gave him her heart.

"A liberal hand! The hearts of old gave hands"

People generally give their hearts to each other when they join hands in marriage but now, they only give their hands away and not their hearts just for some physical pleasure.

OTHELLO
What promise, chuck?
DESDEMONA
I have sent to bid Cassio come speak with you.
OTHELLO
I have a salt and sorry rheum offends me.
Lend me thy handkerchief.
DESDEMONA
Here, my lord.
OTHELLO
That which I gave you.
DESDEMONA
I have it not about me.
OTHELLO
Not?
DESDEMONA
No, faith, my lord.
OTHELLO
That's a fault. That handkerchief
Did an Egyptian to my mother give.
She was a charmer, and could almost read
The thoughts of people.
She told her, while she kept it,
'Twould make her amiable and subdue my father
Entirely to her love. But if she lost it,
Or made a gift of it, my father's eye
Should hold her loathed, and his spirits should hunt
After new fancies. She, dying, gave it me,
And bid me, when my fate would have me wived,
To give it her. I did so; and take heed on 't,
Make it a darling like your precious eye.
To lose 't or give 't away were such perdition
As nothing else could match.
DESDEMONA
Is 't possible?
OTHELLO
'Tis true. There's magic in the web of it.
A sybil that had numbered in the world
The sun to course two hundred compasses,
In her prophetic fury sewed the work.
The worms were hallowed that did breed the silk,
And it was dyed in mummy, which the skilful
Conserved of maidens' hearts.
DESDEMONA
I' faith, is 't true?
OTHELLO
Most veritable. Therefore, look to 't well.
DESDEMONA
Then would to God that I had never seen 't!

He asks Desdemona for the handkerchief he gave her, but she says that she doesn't have it.

Othello is alarmed and he gives her a little anecdote of how he first acquired the handkerchief and how it contained supernatural powers, and that it's former owner was a witch who gave it to his mother.

If she kept it, his father would love her totally but if she lost it his father would loathe her and he will go after other women.

She gave it to him on her deathbed and

"To lose' it or to give it away were such perdition As nothing else could match."

Desdemona is shocked to hear that there's magic sewn into the fabric of the handkerchief.

It was also dyed with the fluid made from preserved virgins' hearts.

The virgin is a reference to Desdemona's purity regarding her marriage.

Ironically, Othello talks of a web, unbeknown to him he is so tightly woven into Iago's deadly web.

TEXT ACT 3 scene 4

OTHELLO
Ha? Wherefore?
DESDEMONA
Why do you speak so startingly and rash?
OTHELLO
Is 't lost? Is 't gone? Speak, is 't out o' th' way?
DESDEMONA
Heaven bless us!
OTHELLO
Say you?
DESDEMONA
It is not lost, but what an if it were?
OTHELLO
How?
DESDEMONA
I say it is not lost.
OTHELLO
Fetch 't. Let me see 't!
DESDEMONA
Why, so I can. But I will not now.
This is a trick to put me from my suit.
Pray you, let Cassio be received again.
OTHELLO
Fetch me the handkerchief!
Aside. My mind misgives
DESDEMONA
Come, come.
You'll never meet a more sufficient man.
OTHELLO
The handkerchief!
DESDEMONA
I pray, talk me of Cassio.
OTHELLO
The handkerchief!
DESDEMONA
A man that all his time
Hath founded his good fortunes on your love;
Shared dangers with you—
OTHELLO
The handkerchief!
DESDEMONA
I' faith, you are to blame.
OTHELLO
Zounds!

OTHELLO *exits*

EMILIA
Is not this man jealous?
DESDEMONA
I ne'er saw this before.
Sure, there's some wonder in this handkerchief!
I am most unhappy in the loss of it.

EXPLANATION

Othello is rude to Desdemona, and she is surprised,

"Why do you speak so startingly and rash?"

Othello's repeated use of rhetorical questions,

"Is 't lost? Is 't gone? Speak, is 't out o' th' way?"

suggests his fractured, tormented mind.

Shakespeare uses a very effective technique in the conversation between Othello and Desdemona.

Othello's combative frame of mind seems to clash with Desdemona's persuasive frame of mind.

He's only interested in the handkerchief as seen in his repeated angry yells, the handkerchief! The handkerchief! The exclamation suggesting his mounting fury. But she is 'adding fuel to the fire' by repeatedly interrupting him with Cassio's reinstatement.

"You'll never meet a more sufficient man."

Desdemona lied about not losing the handkerchief. She is shocked at Othello's rude attitude. She is very confused at this change in his character.

"you are to blame"

Emilia is wise enough to detect Othello's jealousy,

"Is not this man jealous?"

Desdemona expresses her grief at losing the handkerchief.

Emilia is wise enough to detect Othello's jealousy,

"Is not this man jealous?"

Desdemona expresses her grief at losing the handkerchief.

EMILIA
'Tis not a year or two shows us a man.
They are all but stomachs, and we all but food;
They eat us hungerly, and when they are full
They belch us.

Enter
IAGO *and* CASSIO

Look you—Cassio and my husband.
IAGO, *to Cassio*
There is no other way; 'tis she must do 't,
And, lo, the happiness! Go and importune her.
DESDEMONA
How now, good Cassio, what's the news with you?
CASSIO
Madam, my former suit. I do beseech you
That by your virtuous means I may again
Exist, and be a member of his love
Whom I with all the office of my heart
Entirely honour. I would not be delayed.
If my offense be of such mortal kind
That nor my service past nor present sorrows
Nor purposed merit in futurity
Can ransom me into his love again,
But to know so must be my benefit.
So shall I clothe me in a forced content,
And shut myself up in some other course.
To fortune's alms.
DESDEMONA
Alas, thrice-gentle Cassio,
My advocation is not now in tune.
My lord is not my lord; nor should I know him
Were he in favour as in humour altered.
So help me every spirit sanctified
As I have spoken for you all my best,
And stood within the blank of his displeasure
For my free speech! You must awhile be patient.
What I can do I will; and more I will
Than for myself I dare. Let that suffice you.
IAGO
Is my lord angry?
EMILIA
He went hence but now,
And certainly in strange unquietness.
IAGO
Can he be angry? I have seen the cannon
When it hath blown his ranks into the air
And, like the devil, from his very arm
Puffed his own brother—and is he angry?
Something of moment then. I will go meet him.
There's matter in 't indeed if he be angry.

It's no more a symbol of love but ominously a symbol of destruction. Emilia uses a vivid imagery to describe man's ugliness. We are food, they eat us hungrily and vomit us.

Iago's cynical and obnoxious behaviour continues. Cassio is like, 'a lamb to the slaughter.'

He still allows himself to be played by Iago. He is forced to confront Desdemona for his job. By now we are beginning to empathise with Desdemona's plight. She is unwittingly falling prey to Iago's devious trap.

Cassio pours out his heart to her. He wants to be in Othello's favour again.

"Can ransom me into his love again"

If he is unsuccessful then he will find another job.

Desdemona very gently waives Cassio away telling him that Othello is behaving strangely,

"My Lord is not my Lord"

She spoke sincerely on his behalf but that only angered Othello,

"And stood within the blank of his displeasure For my free speech!"

Cassio will have to wait. Iago is wielding his vile influence again.

He insists that Othello never gets angry in any circumstance.

He remained calm and calculated in the face of danger in the war when his soldiers were being blown to bits.

Ironically, Iago compares him to the devil.

We are now losing our sympathy for Othello because of his dark, evil thoughts. Even Desdemona puts her faith in Iago and asks him to console Othello.

DESDEMONA
I prithee do so.

IAGO ***exits***

Something, sure, of state,
Either from Venice, or some unhatched practice
Made demonstrable here in Cyprus to him,
Hath puddled his clear spirit; and in such cases
Men's natures wrangle with inferior things,
Though great ones are their object. 'Tis even so.
For let our finger ache, and it endues
Our other healthful members even to a sense
Of pain. Nay, we must think men are not gods,
Nor of them look for such observancy
As fits the bridal. Beshrew me much, Emilia,
I was—unhandsome warrior as I am!—
Arraigning his unkindness with my soul.
But now I find I had suborned the witness,
And he's indicted falsely.

EMILIA
Pray heaven it be
State matters, as you think, and no conception
Nor no jealous toy concerning you.

DESDEMONA
Alas the day, I never gave him cause!

EMILIA
But jealous souls will not be answered so.
They are not ever jealous for the cause,
But jealous for they're jealous. It is a monster
Begot upon itself, born on itself.

DESDEMONA
Heaven keep that monster from Othello's mind!

EMILIA
Lady, amen.

DESDEMONA
I will go seek him.—Cassio, walk hereabout.
If I do find him fit, I'll move your suit
And seek to effect it to my uttermost.

CASSIO
I humbly thank your Ladyship.

She is convinced that some urgent state business from Venice or something sinister here in Cyprus is troubling Othello.

She ominously mentioned 'unhatched practice'. Which can be referred to Iago's deadly plot of jealousy and destruction.

She still makes excuses for Othello blaming herself for misunderstanding him.

"And he's indicted falsely."

The audience has become nervous for Desdemona because she proves to be the perfect heroine – innocent and kind but a pawn in a deadly game.

Emilia insists that Othello is jealous, but Desdemona says,

"I never gave him cause."

Desdemona is very perceptive. She creates a visual imagery using a biblical reference.

"Heaven keep that monster from Othello's mind."

It's true the monster Iago has taken full control and manipulated Othello's mind.

He had crushed his spirit and is slowly dissolving his marriage.

DESDEMONA *and* EMILIA *exit*

***Enter* BIANCA**

BIANCA
'Save you, friend Cassio!
CASSIO
What make you from home?
How is 't with you, my most fair Bianca?
I' faith, sweet love, I was coming to your house.
BIANCA
And I was going to your lodging, Cassio.
What, keep a week away? Seven days and nights,
Eightscore eight hours, and lovers' absent hours
More tedious than the dial eightscore times?
O weary reck'ning!
CASSIO
Pardon me, Bianca.
I have this while with leaden thoughts been pressed,
But I shall in a more continuate time
Strike off this score of absence. Sweet Bianca,
Giving her Desdemona's handkerchief
Take me this work out.
BIANCA
O, Cassio, whence came this?
This is some token from a newer friend.
To the felt absence now I feel a cause.
Is 't come to this? Well, well.
CASSIO
Go to, woman!
Throw your vile guesses in the devil's teeth,
From whence you have them. You are jealous now
That this is from some mistress,
Some remembrance.
No, by my faith, Bianca.
BIANCA
Why, whose is it?
CASSIO
I know not neither. I found it in my chamber.
I like the work well. Ere it be demanded,
As like enough it will, I would have it copied.
Take it, and do 't, and leave me for this time.
BIANCA
Leave you? Wherefore?
CASSIO
I do attend here on the General,
And think it no addition, nor my wish,
To have him see me womaned.
BIANCA
Why, I pray you?
CASSIO
Not that I love you not.

We are introduced to Bianca for the first time. She creates more intricacies and weaves more problems into an already troubled plot.

She is Cassio's mistress, and she adds to his misery by accusing him of neglect, but we know that his plate was full of problems.

He very innocently gives her the handkerchief and asks her to copy the pretty pattern for him. She becomes irate and accuses him of obtaining it from a new girlfriend.

"This is some token from a newer friend."

He is angry with her,

"Go to, woman!"

Notice how Shakespeare presents conflicts in all the relationships in the play. It is a foreshadowing of the disastrous breakdown of the loving relationship between Othello and Desdemona.

Bianca's suspicions here mirrors Othello's suspicions and just like Othello, Cassio gets irritated and asks Bianca to,

"leave me for this time"

In Act 3 scene 3 line 97, Othello too says,

"Farewell my Desdemona. I'll come to thee straight."

Cassio tells Bianca that he doesn't know whose handkerchief it was and that he found it in his chamber.

He is waiting for Othello and ironically, he doesn't want him to see him with a woman.

"To have him see me womaned."

Actually, Othello wouldn't mind seeing him with a woman as long as it is not his Desdemona.

BIANCA
But that you do not love me!
I pray you bring me on the way a little,
And say if I shall see you soon at night.
CASSIO
'Tis but a little way that I can bring you,
For I attend here. But I'll see you soon.
BIANCA
'Tis very good. I must be circumstanced.

THEY ***exit***

Note also how submissive the women have to be. Although she didn't like being side-stepped, she has to contend with it.

"Tis very good. I must be circumstanced."

ACT 4

SUMMARY

In scene 1

- Iago taunts Othello with vile images of Cassio and Desdemona together and he plants the notion of infidelity in his head. Othello has lost all sense of reasoning because of his fury and he falls into a fit.
- Cassio enters and notices Othello's pathetic state, but Iago convinces him that he is taking care of Othello.
- Iago is incorrigible, he wants to torment Othello further and asks him to withdraw and listen to his conversation with Cassio. He will question Cassio about Bianca and laugh, and this will make Othello misinterpret it as being Desdemona that they are talking about. This will infuriate Othello, and this will serve as a confirmation of Desdemona's betrayal with Cassio.
- To add 'fuel to the fire' Bianca enters sporting Desdemona's handkerchief. On seeing it Othello becomes livid with rage.
- He decides to kill both Cassio and Desdemona, but evil Iago tells him to kill Desdemona in her bed. He also agrees to kill Cassio for Othello.
- Lord Lodovico enters with Desdemona who brings news that Cassio is to replace Othello.
- When Desdemona revisits her pleas about Cassio, Othello becomes furious, and he strikes her.
- Lodovico is shocked at Othello's crass behaviour and Iago tells him about Othello's behaviour that he has just noticed inside.

In scene 2

- Othello questions Emilia about the relationship between Desdemona and Cassio and she is honestly forthright in saying that it was just an innocent platonic relationship and nothing sexual.
- Sadly though, Othello doubts her honesty.
- When Desdemona enters Othello hurls a tirade of abuse at her. He calls her a 'whore'.
- Desdemona is shocked at Othello's behaviour and she urges Iago to reason with him and maybe alter his foul mood.
- Roderigo is very irate with Iago and he threatens him that he will go to Desdemona to retrieve his jewellery and money.
- Iago enlists Roderigo on his malicious plot to kill Cassio saying that he will realise the benefit it will have for him in getting Desdemona.

In scene 3

- Othello commands Desdemona to go to bed and he walks out with Lodovico. Desdemona says that despite Othello's violent behaviour, she still loves him. The women talk about women being unfaithful to their husbands, something that Desdemona cannot imagine.
- Desdemona just simply cannot erase a very melancholy song that Barbary sang before her death.
- She bids Emilia goodnight.

Before the Citadel

Enter
OTHELLO *and* LAGO

IAGO
Will you think so?
OTHELLO
Think so, Iago?
IAGO
What,
To kiss in private?
OTHELLO
An unauthorized kiss!
IAGO
Or to be naked with her friend in bed
An hour or more, not meaning any harm?
OTHELLO
Naked in bed, Iago, and not mean harm?
It is hypocrisy against the devil!
They that mean virtuously, and yet do so,
The devil their virtue tempts,
And they tempt heaven.
IAGO
If they do nothing, 'tis a venial slip.
But if I give my wife a handkerchief—
OTHELLO
What then?
IAGO
Why then, 'tis hers, my lord, and being hers,
She may, I think, bestow 't on any man.
OTHELLO
She is protectress of her honour, too.
May she give that?
IAGO
Her honour is an essence that's not seen;
They have it very oft that have it not.
But for the handkerchief—
OTHELLO
By heaven, I would most gladly have forgot it.
Thou saidst—O, it comes o'er my memory
As doth the raven o'er the infectious house,
Boding to all—he had my handkerchief.
IAGO
Ay, what of that?
OTHELLO
That's not so good now.
But they must blab—

Othello is spiralling downward, and sadistic Iago is unrelenting in his pursuit of revenge because he creates a vulgar, debase, lewd imagery of Desdemona and Cassio being in bed and kissing. Iago is now in total control of Othello's mind and thoughts.

Note the use of short, snappy questions which increases the pace because Iago wants the action to move on quickly to achieve his evil goals.

Othello mentions the devil twice,

"It is hypocrisy against the devil!"

Ironically, both Iago and Othello are evil like the devil. They think devious thoughts. They are so consumed with hate, anger and revenge that will ultimately destroy them. Iago goads Othello on, 'rubbing salt in his wounds' telling him that Desdemona has a right to give the handkerchief to any man because it belongs to her.

She can even give her honour to any man if she wishes,

"She is a protectress of her honour, too."

The memory of the handkerchief is haunting Othello. He hates the fact that it is in Cassio's possession.

"O, it comes o'er my memory
As doth the raven o'er the infectious house"

The raven is said to be a bird of ill omen and it signifies death which can foreshadow Othello's evil intentions of death.

Iago further taunts Othello of how men blab and scandalise the women they have affairs with.

IAGO
What
If I had said I had seen him do you wrong?
Or heard him say (as knaves be such abroad,
Who having, by their own importunate suit
Or voluntary dotage of some mistress,
Convincèd or supplied them, cannot choose

OTHELLO
Hath he said anything?

IAGO
He hath, my lord, but be you well assured,
No more than he'll unswear.

OTHELLO
What hath he said?

IAGO
Faith, that he did—I know not what he did.

OTHELLO
What? What?

IAGO
Lie—

OTHELLO
With her?

IAGO
With her—on her—what you will.

OTHELLO
Lie with her? Lie on her? We say "lie on her" when they belie her. Lie with her—Zounds, that's fulsome! Handkerchief—confessions—handkerchief. To confess and be hanged for his labour. First to be hanged and then to confess—I tremble at it. Nature would not invest herself in such shadowing passion without some instruction. It is not words that shakes me thus. Pish! Noses, ears, and lips—is 't possible? Confess—handkerchief—O, devil!

HE ***falls into a trance***

IAGO
Work on,
My medicine, work!
Thus credulous fools are caught,
And many worthy and chaste dames even thus,
All guiltless, meet reproach.—What ho! My lord!
My lord, I say. Othello!

Enter **CASSIO**

How now, Cassio?

CASSIO
What's the matter?

EXPLANATION

Othello takes the bait, and he wants to know more about what Cassio said. Iago feeds his growing appetite for revenge and he starts the conversation but withdraws the information,

"Faith, that he did – I know not what he did."

It's a scheming ploy Iago uses to get his victims hooked.

Iago pretends and hesitates – note his use of hyphens suggesting his pauses, when he lies to Othello that Cassio told him that, he was in bed with her. Notice how Othello completes Iago's sentence, 'with her.'

One can infer that they have become one because of their mutual 'respect and love' for each other. Othello is furious, this speech is very emotional and heart-wrenching.

The use of the punctuation - rhetorical questions, hyphens, direct speech, repetitions and exclamations all denotes Othello's complete breakdown.

His pain and agony have now reached 'boiling point' and his rage is uncontrollable.

The constant repetition of, "lie with her" Sends him into a frenzy and he's now determined to kill Cassio.

He falls into a trance. Iago is thrilled and he calls him Othello showing his disrespect.

TEXT ACT 4 scene 1

IAGO
My lord is fall'n into an epilepsy.
This is his second fit. He had one yesterday.
CASSIO
Rub him about the temples.
IAGO
No, forbear.
The lethargy must have his quiet course.
If not, he foams at mouth, and by and by
Breaks out to savage madness. Look, he stirs.
Do you withdraw yourself a little while.
He will recover straight. When he is gone,
I would on great occasion speak with you.

CASSIO ***exits***

How is it, general? Have you not hurt your head?
OTHELLO
Dost thou mock me?
IAGO
I mock you not, by heaven!
Would you would bear your fortune like a man!
OTHELLO
A hornèd man's a monster and a beast.
IAGO
There's many a beast, then, in a populous city,
And many a civil monster.
OTHELLO
Did he confess it?
IAGO
Good sir, be a man!
Think every bearded fellow that's but yoked
May draw with you. There's millions now alive
That nightly lie in those unproper beds
Which they dare swear peculiar. Your case is better.
O, 'tis the spite of hell, the fiend's arch-mock,
To lip a wanton in a secure couch
And to suppose her chaste! No, let me know,
And knowing what I am, I know what she shall be.
OTHELLO
O, thou art wise, 'tis certain.

EXPLANATION

Iago's narcissist and sadistic nature is shocking, he is enjoying Othello's suffering. Cassio even suggests some treatment, but he refused to administer it but makes this terrible comment instead,

"Breaks out to savage madness."

The audience has now become captivated with Iago because his maliciousness transcends all human boundaries.

Shakespeare has created a unique character whose ingenious, vile plans fits in like a 'jigsaw puzzle.'

Iago asks Othello to be a man and face his problems stoically.

"Would you would bear your fortune like a man!"

Iago's appetite for human suffering and destruction is monumental,

"There's many a beast, then, in a populous city, And many a civil monster."

These are Iago's words which can aptly describe his character.

IAGO
Stand you awhile apart.
Confine yourself but in a patient list.
Whilst you were here, o'erwhelmèd with your grief
A passion most unsuiting such a man—
Cassio came hither. I shifted him away
And laid good 'scuses upon your ecstasy,
Bade him anon return and here speak with me,
The which he promised. Do but encave yourself,
And mark the fleers, the gibes, and notable scorns
That dwell in every region of his face.
For I will make him tell the tale anew—
Where, how, how oft, how long ago, and when
He hath and is again to cope your wife.
I say but mark his gesture. Marry, patience,
Or I shall say you're all in all in spleen,
And nothing of a man.

OTHELLO
Dost thou hear, Iago,
I will be found most cunning in my patience,
But - dost thou hear? - most bloody.

IAGO
That's not amiss.
But yet keep time in all. Will you withdraw?

OTHELLO ***withdraws***

Now will I question Cassio of Bianca,
A huswife that by selling her desires
Buys herself bread and clothes. It is a creature
That dotes on Cassio—as 'tis the strumpet's plague
To beguile many and be beguiled by one.
He, when he hears of her, cannot restrain
From the excess of laughter. Here he comes.

Enter **CASSIO**

As he shall smile, Othello shall go mad,
And his unbookish jealousy must construe
Poor Cassio's smiles, gestures, and light behaviours
Quite in the wrong.—How do you, lieutenant?

CASSIO
The worser that you give me the addition
Whose want even kills me.

IAGO
Ply Desdemona well, and you are sure on 't.
Now, if this suit lay in Bianca's power,
How quickly should you speed!

CASSIO, *laughing*
Alas, poor caitiff!

OTHELLO
Look how he laughs already!

Iago commands Othello's every move – his thoughts and his imagination. Othello is now like a puppet. He still believes that Iago is 'wise' and Iago is thoroughly enjoying his sense of power. He directs Othello to go somewhere and cool off and remarks that Othello's overwhelming sense of passion is unbecoming for a man of his status.

"O'erwhelmed with your grief
A passion most unsuiting such a man."

Iago lies that Cassio came and saw him in his sorry state and he made some good excuses to uphold his dignity, which was certainly not the case. He orders Othello to hide so that he can hear Cassio reveal every detail about his affair with Desdemona.

Othello talks about being 'bloody' with Cassio and taking revenge.

Iago's misogynistic behaviour surfaces once more when he degrades Bianca for her loose way of living.

He plans to discuss her with Cassio, fooling Othello into thinking that they are discussing Cassio 's sordid affair with Desdemona.

"As he shall smile, Othello shall go mad"

Othello is totally ignorant of what is happening so he will sink into the deepest depths of despair.

Everything goes as Iago planned. He tells Cassio to persist in asking Desdemona for his job and he'll get it back.

IAGO
I never knew woman love man so.
CASSIO
Alas, poor rogue, I think i' faith she loves me.
OTHELLO
Now he denies it faintly and laughs it out.
IAGO
Do you hear, Cassio?
OTHELLO
Now he importunes him
To tell it o'er. Go to, well said, well said.
IAGO
She gives it out that you shall marry her.
Do you intend it?
CASSIO
Ha, ha, ha!
OTHELLO
Do you triumph, Roman? Do you triumph?
CASSIO
I marry her? What, a customer? Prithee bear some
charity to my wit! Do not think it so unwholesome.
Ha, ha, ha!
OTHELLO
So, so, so, so. They laugh that wins.
IAGO
Faith, the cry goes that you marry her.
CASSIO
Prithee say true!
IAGO
I am a very villain else.
OTHELLO
Have you scored me? Well.
CASSIO
This is the monkey's own giving out. She is
persuaded I will marry her out of her own love and
flattery, not out of my promise.
OTHELLO
Iago beckons me. Now he begins the story.
CASSIO
She was here even now. She haunts me in every
place. I was the other day talking on the sea-bank
with certain Venetians, and thither comes the
bauble. By this hand, she falls thus about my neck!
OTHELLO
Crying, "O dear Cassio," as it were,
His gesture imports it.
CASSIO
So hangs and lolls and weeps upon me,
So shakes and pulls me. Ha, ha, ha!

Othello is livid that Cassio is laughing, and his imagination goes wild, and he concocts some wild ideas thinking it's about Desdemona.

"Now he denies it faintly and laughs it out."

Iago very craftily makes jokes about Bianca marrying Cassio and Cassio laughs about it.

Out of interest it's nice to see the juxtaposition of Cassio's attitude to Desdemona, who he had the utmost respect for compared to that of Bianca,

"I marry her? What, a customer? Prithee bear some charity to my wit!"

He shares almost the same derogatory view of women like Iago. This shows how women were treated as commodities to be owned in the Renaissance era.

Othello is seething, his fury is mounting,

"So, so, so, so. They laugh that wins."

Othello is getting all wound up.

Cassio tells in detail how Bianca,

"haunts me in every place"

and he is very expressive in his gestures and Othello thinks that it is Desdemona who is performing these acts with Cassio.

OTHELLO
Now he tells how she plucked him to my chamber.
O, I see that nose of yours,
but not that dog I shall throw it to.

CASSIO
Well, I must leave her company.

IAGO
Before me, look where she comes.

***Enter* BIANCA**

CASSIO
'Tis such another fitchew—marry, a perfumed one!
What do you mean by this haunting of me?

BIANCA
Let the devil and his dam haunt you! What did
you mean by that same handkerchief you gave me
even now? I was a fine fool to take it! I must take
out the work? A likely piece of work, that you
should find it in your chamber and know not who
left it there! This is some minx's token, and I must
take out the work! There, give it your hobbyhorse.
Wheresoever you had it, I'll take out no work on 't.

CASSIO
How now, my sweet Bianca? How now? How now?

OTHELLO
By heaven, that should be my handkerchief!

BIANCA
If you'll come to supper tonight you may.
If you will not, come when you are next prepared for

SHE *exits*

IAGO
After her, after her!

CASSIO
Faith, I must. She'll rail in the streets else.

IAGO
Will you sup there?

CASSIO
Faith, I intend so.

IAGO
Well, I may chance to see you,
For I would very fain speak with you.

CASSIO
Prithee come. Will you?

IAGO
Go to; say no more.

CASSIO *exits*

He is degrading himself even further with these crazy thoughts. Now he imagines that Desdemona took Cassio into their bedroom,

"plucked him to my chamber."

Sweet revenge is in his mind. Cassio laughs, and degrades Bianca but ironically, he is the fool who is being laughed at by Iago.

He's taken in 'hook, line, and sinker' by Iago. Bianca comes in with the handkerchief and has a tantrum because she firmly believes that the handkerchief came from another lover,

"This is some minx's token"

Surprisingly Cassio mirrors Iago in some respects – a two faced fool. He just called Bianca a whore and he speaks with a forked tongue like Iago. Now when he sees her, he addresses her thus,

"How now, my sweet Bianca?"

Speaking with a silver tongue and a loving tone. Othello sees the handkerchief and he is perplexed,

"By heaven, that should be my handkerchief!"

Now he got confirmation.

OTHELLO, *coming forward*
How shall I murder him, Iago?
IAGO
Did you perceive how he laughed at his vice?
OTHELLO
O Iago!
IAGO
And did you see the handkerchief?
OTHELLO
Was that mine?
IAGO
Yours, by this hand! And to see
How he prizes the foolish woman your wife!
She gave it him, and he hath giv'n it his whore.
OTHELLO
I would have him nine years a-killing!
A fine woman, a fair woman, a sweet woman!
IAGO
Nay, you must forget that.
OTHELLO
Ay, let her rot and perish and be damned tonight,
for she shall not live. No, my heart is turned to
stone. I strike it, and it hurts my hand. O, the world
hath not a sweeter creature! She might lie by an
emperor's side and command him tasks.
IAGO
Nay, that's not your way.
OTHELLO
Hang her, I do but say what she is!
So delicate with her needle, an admirable musician
O, she will sing the savageness out of a bear!
Of so high and plenteous wit and invention!
IAGO
She's the worse for all this.
OTHELLO
O, a thousand, a thousand times!—
And then of so gentle a condition!
IAGO
Ay, too gentle.
OTHELLO
Nay, that's certain. But yet the pity of it, Iago!
O, Iago, the pity of it, Iago!
IAGO
If you are so fond over her iniquity,
Give her patent to offend,
For if it touch not you, it comes near nobody.
OTHELLO
I will chop her into messes! Cuckold me?
IAGO
O, 'tis foul in her.
OTHELLO
With mine officer!

The action has now reached new heights. Othello's faculties have taken leave of him. Our hero has now reached a shocking level of degradation. He is bent on murder. He asks Iago for ways to kill Cassio

"How shall I murder him, Iago?"

We have to compare Othello - the upstanding, moral, respected army general to this raving lunatic who has lost his senses because of his anger and jealousy.

He plans to kill his wife. His untold rage is seen in the onomatopoeia,

"let her rot and perish and be damned tonight, for she shall not live"

The audience has lost all respect and sympathy for Othello.

He has now become the antagonist and claims that his heart is turned to stone.

Othello is harbouring barbaric thoughts of killing. He is deciding to hang his wife. This violent imagery is shocking, and it highlights Othello's deranged mental state.

"I will chop her into messes! Cuckold me?"

IAGO
That's fouler.
OTHELLO
Get me some poison, Iago, this night. I'll not
expostulate with her lest her body and beauty
unprovide my mind again. This night, Iago.
IAGO
Do it not with poison. Strangle her in her bed,
even the bed she hath contaminated.
OTHELLO
Good, good. The justice of it pleases. Very good.
IAGO
And for Cassio, let me be his undertaker.
You shall hear more by midnight.
OTHELLO
Excellent good.

A trumpet sounds

What trumpet is that same?
IAGO
I warrant something from Venice.
'Tis Lodovico. This comes from the Duke.
See, your wife's with him.

Enter
LODOVICO, DESDEMONA, ***and Attendants***

LODOVICO
God save you, worthy general.
OTHELLO
With all my heart, sir.
LODOVICO
The Duke and the Senators of Venice greet you.
HE ***hands*** **OTHELLO** ***a paper.***

OTHELLO
I kiss the instrument of their pleasures.
DESDEMONA
And what's the news, good cousin Lodovico?
IAGO
I am very glad to see you, signior.
Welcome to Cyprus.
LODOVICO
I thank you. How does Lieutenant Cassio?
IAGO
Lives, sir.

He asks Iago for poison, but Iago wants to take full control of the action and he cruelly suggests,

"Strangle her in her bed,
even the bed she hath contaminated."

It's disconcerting to see how Othello has allowed Iago to destroy him.

The sound of the trumpet is symbolic, it can signify Iago's jubilance at his success thus far.

Lodovico arrives from Venice with news from the Duke. Iago's zest for causing trouble is insatiable.

He immediately directs Othello to the fact that Desdemona is in Lodovico's company implying that she likes to be in the company of other men.

There is a very tense atmosphere when Lodovico arrives.

It's also riddled with suspense because we are well aware of Othello's volatile state of mind.

To add 'fuel to the fire,' Lodovico brought news that Cassio was requested to replace Othello as general. This is sure going to enrage Othello knowing full well the intense hate that he is harbouring for Cassio.

DESDEMONA
Cousin, there's fall'n between him and my lord
An unkind breach, but you shall make all well.
OTHELLO
Are you sure of that?
DESDEMONA
My lord?
OTHELLO*, reading*
"This fail you not to do, as you will"—
LODOVICO
He did not call; he's busy in the paper.
Is there division 'twixt my lord and Cassio?
DESDEMONA
A most unhappy one. I would do much
T' atone them, for the love I bear to Cassio.
OTHELLO
Fire and brimstone!
DESDEMONA
My lord?
OTHELLO
Are you wise?
DESDEMONA
What, is he angry?
LODOVICO
May be the letter moved him.
For, as I think, they do command him home,
Deputing Cassio in his government.
DESDEMONA
By my troth, I am glad on 't.
OTHELLO
Indeed?
DESDEMONA
My lord?
OTHELLO
Are you wise?
DESDEMONA
What, is he angry?
LODOVICO
May be the letter moved him.
For, as I think, they do command him home,
Deputing Cassio in his government.
DESDEMONA
By my troth, I am glad on 't.
OTHELLO
Indeed?
DESDEMONA
My lord?
OTHELLO
I am glad to see you mad.

To make matters even worse, Desdemona intervenes and tells Lodovico that there is a serious rift between Othello and Cassio which he must fix.

"there's fall'n between him and my lord,
An unkind breach, but you shall make all well"

She also innocently remarked,

"for the love I bear to Cassio."

She also said that she is happy that Cassio got the job as governor.

Obviously, this sent Othello into a fitful rage, and he yells out,

"Fire and brimstone!"

This biblical imagery is associated with hell and the punishment sinners received.

Ironically, Othello is securing a comfortable niche there.

DESDEMONA
Why, sweet Othello!
OTHELLO, *striking her*
Devil!
DESDEMONA
I have not deserved this.
LODOVICO
My lord, this would not be believed in Venice,
Though I should swear I saw 't. 'Tis very much.
Make her amends. She weeps.
OTHELLO
O, devil, devil!
If that the Earth could teem with woman's tears,
Each drop she falls would prove a crocodile.
Out of my sight!
DESDEMONA
I will not stay to offend you.

DESDEMONA ***begins to leave***

LODOVICO
Truly an obedient lady.
I do beseech your Lordship call her back.
OTHELLO
Mistress.
DESDEMONA, *turning back*
My lord?
OTHELLO
What would you with her, sir?
LODOVICO
Who, I, my lord?
OTHELLO
Ay, you did wish that I would make her turn.
Sir, she can turn, and turn, and yet go on,
And turn again. And she can weep, sir, weep.
And she's obedient, as you say, obedient.
Very obedient.—Proceed you in your tears.—
Concerning this, sir—O, well-painted passion!—
I am commanded home.—Get you away.
I'll send for you anon.—Sir, I obey the mandate
And will return to Venice.—Hence, avaunt!

DESDEMONA ***exits***

Cassio shall have my place. And, sir, tonight
I do entreat that we may sup together.
You are welcome, sir, to Cyprus.
Goats and monkeys!

OTHELLO ***exits***

She is shocked and confused at his reaction and she innocently and lovingly, responds,

"Why, sweet Othello!"

He strikes her in front of the guest and her only response is,

"I have not deserved this."

Now our hearts go out to Desdemona to be humiliated like that in public. Lodovico is astounded at what he witnessed, and he asks Othello to apologise. He calls her the 'devil' and so rudely dismisses her.

"Out of my sight!"

Sadly, she is still obedient to her husband and says,

"I will not stay to offend you."

The verb 'obedience' is repeated many times. Women were expected to be obedient and subservient to their husbands.

Despite her being brutalized by this savage behaviour, she is still obedient and answers him politely when he called her, 'My lord' and she turned to face him.

Othello is lewd when he refers to 'turn' repeatedly, making suggestion to her 'affair'.

Othello is complaining profusely about his wife to Lodovico. He is very cold and passionate in his deliverance.

The many hyphens show the breaks in his speech, this can be a reflection of his fractured, broken mind.

The hyphens can also suggest that he is trying to control his passion and his conflicting feelings of hate and love for Desdemona.

Lodovico is in total shock at what he is witnessing. He just cannot believe the terrible drastic change in Othello.

TEXT ACT 4 scene 1

LODOVICO
Is this the noble Moor, whom our full senate
Call all in all sufficient? Is this the nature
Whom passion could not shake, whose solid virtue
The shot of accident nor dart of chance
Could neither graze nor pierce?
IAGO
He is much changed.
LODOVICO
Are his wits safe? Is he not light of brain?
IAGO
He's that he is. I may not breathe my censure
What he might be. If what he might he is not,
I would to heaven he were.
LODOVICO
What? Strike his wife?
IAGO
'Faith, that was not so well. Yet would I knew
That stroke would prove the worst.
LODOVICO
Is it his use?
Or did the letters work upon his blood
And new-create this fault?
IAGO
Alas, alas!
It is not honesty in me to speak
What I have seen and known.
You shall observe him,
And his own courses will denote him so
That I may save my speech. Do but go after
And mark how he continues.
LODOVICO
I am sorry that I am deceived in him.

THEY ***exit***

EXPLANATION

The use of the repeated questioning shows us his disbelief, that a celebrated war hero can behave in such a despicable manner.

"Is this the noble Moor"

Lodovico asks Iago if Othello is losing his mind, but Iago's response was shocking.

He says he wishes that it is the last time that Othello strikes his wife.

He also says that he cannot tell him everything he's seen and heard.

He asks Lodovico to carefully observe Othello's actions and he would see what a terrible person he is.

"Do but go after
And mark how he continues."
"

Lodovico is disgusted at what he hears, and he is so regretful that he was deceived.

"I am sorry that I am deceived in him."

A Room in the Citadel

Enter
OTHELLO *and* EMILIA

OTHELLO
You have seen nothing then?
EMILIA
Nor ever heard, nor ever did suspect.
OTHELLO
Yes, you have seen Cassio and she together.
EMILIA
But then I saw no harm, and then I heard
Each syllable that breath made up between them.
OTHELLO
What, did they never whisper?
EMILIA
Never, my lord.
OTHELLO
Nor send you out o' th' way?
EMILIA
Never.
OTHELLO
To fetch her fan, her gloves, her mask, nor nothing?
EMILIA
Never, my lord.
OTHELLO
That's strange.
EMILIA
I durst, my lord, to wager she is honest,
Lay down my soul at stake. If you think other,
Remove your thought. It doth abuse your bosom.
If any wretch have put this in your head,
Let heaven requite it with the serpent's curse,
For if she be not honest, chaste, and true,
There's no man happy. The purest of their wives
Is foul as slander.
OTHELLO
Bid her come hither. Go.

EMILIA *exits*

She says enough. Yet she's a simple bawd
That cannot say as much. This is a subtle whore,
A closet lock and key of villainous secrets.
And yet she'll kneel and pray. I have seen her do 't.

Othello is still unconvinced that Desdemona is unfaithful to him. He wants reassurance from Emilia.

She is a faithful and trusted servant but sadly became an unwitting pawn in Iago's deadly game.

Othello questions her at length about the relationship between his wife and Cassio but she is adamant that the relationship was platonic and nothing physical.

Note that during this conversation Othello's speech is peppered with mainly questions as though egging Emilia on to say that he is right in his suspicions,

"What did they never whisper?"

Shakespeare uses dramatic irony here when Emilia vehemently denies that Desdemona was unfaithful.

'Lay down my soul at stake.'

She urges him to remove this unkindly thought.

Ironically, she unwittingly curses her husband and associates him with the 'serpent', and she asks heaven to curse him for his lies. Othello belittles his wife calling her a 'whore' accusing her of harbouring a closet full of terrible secrets, 'villainous secrets.'

TEXT ACT 4 scene 2

Enter
DESDEMONA *and* EMILIA

DESDEMONA
My lord, what is your will?
OTHELLO
Pray you, chuck, come hither.
DESDEMONA
What is your pleasure?
OTHELLO
Let me see your eyes. Look in my face.
DESDEMONA
What horrible fancy's this?
OTHELLO, *to Emilia*
Some of your function, mistress.
Leave procreants alone, and shut the door.
Cough, or cry "hem," if anybody come.
Your mystery, your mystery! Nay, dispatch.

EMILIA *exits*

DESDEMONA, *kneeling*
Upon my knees, what doth your speech import?
I understand a fury in your words,
But not the words.
OTHELLO
Why? What art thou?
DESDEMONA
Your wife, my lord, your true and loyal wife.
OTHELLO
Come, swear it. Damn thyself,
Lest, being like one of heaven, the devils themselves
Should fear to seize thee.
Therefore be double damned.
Swear thou art honest.
DESDEMONA
Heaven doth truly know it.
OTHELLO
Heaven truly knows that thou art false as hell.
DESDEMONA, *standing*
To whom, my lord? With whom? How am I false?
OTHELLO
Ah, Desdemon, away, away, away!
DESDEMONA
Alas the heavy day, why do you weep?
Am I the motive of these tears, my lord?
If haply you my father do suspect
An instrument of this your calling back,
Lay not your blame on me. If you have lost him,
I have lost him too.

EXPLANATION

There is a sad sense of pathos here when Desdemona enters like, 'a lamb to the slaughter'.

She is so meek and docile after Othello's brutish treatment of her.

The reader empathizes with her, and they get emotionally involved. Desdemona demands to know of his strange behaviour,

'What horrible fancy's this?'

He wants to look into her eyes and her face to see for any guilt.

She goes on her knees and begs him to tell her why he is so curt and rude to her. She dutifully tells him that she is,

"Your wife, my lord, your true and loyal wife"

Othello uses a juxtaposed biblical imagery of heaven and the devils when he accuses Desdemona of being like 'heaven' but he says that the devils would mistake her for an angel and would be afraid to hold her.

This is a reflection of Othello's deranged state of mind. He certainly is acting bitter and vile like the devil.

There's also a repetition of the noun 'heaven' several times and it's rather foreboding and ominous because Desdemona is now on the brink of death and heading towards heaven.

We empathize with Desdmona's plight, and she tugs at our heartstrings.

Her total shock and disbelief at Othello's unfounded accusations is seen in her constant questioning,

"To whom, my lord? With whom? How am I false?"

She is still concerned about him because he is crying.

"why do you weep?"

OTHELLO
Had it pleased heaven
To try me with affliction, had they rained
All kind of sores and shames on my bare head,
Steeped me in poverty to the very lips,
Given to captivity me and my utmost hopes,
I should have found in some place of my soul
A drop of patience. But alas, to make me
A fixèd figure for the time of scorn
To point his slow unmoving finger at—
Yet could I bear that too, well, very well.
But there where I have garnered up my heart,
Where either I must live or bear no life,
The fountain from the which my current runs
Or else dries up—to be discarded thence,
Or keep it as a cistern for foul toads
To knot and gender in—turn thy complexion there,
Patience, thou young and rose-lipped cherubin,
Ay, there look grim as hell.

DESDEMONA
I hope my noble lord esteems me honest.

OTHELLO
O, ay, as summer flies are in the shambles,
That quicken even with blowing! O thou weed,
Who art so lovely fair, and smell'st so sweet
That the sense aches at thee,
Would thou hadst ne'er been born!

DESDEMONA
Alas, what ignorant sin have I committed?

OTHELLO
Was this fair paper, this most goodly book,
Made to write "whore" upon? What committed?
Committed? O thou public commoner,
I should make very forges of my cheeks
That would to cinders burn up modesty,
Did I but speak thy deeds. What committed?
Heaven stops the nose at it, and the moon winks.
The bawdy wind that kisses all it meets
Is hushed within the hollow mine of earth
And will not hear 't. What committed?
Impudent strumpet!

DESDEMONA
By heaven, you do me wrong!

OTHELLO
Are not you a strumpet?

DESDEMONA
No, as I am a Christian!
If to preserve this vessel for my lord
From any other foul unlawful touch
Be not to be a strumpet, I am none.

Othello is using much religious imagery as though blaming God for his pain and he even uses a simile, 'grim as hell' which reflects his current dilemma.

He compares himself to Job in the Bible upon whom God had inflicted terrible, unbearable sores and pain to test his faith in God. Job persevered and got God's blessing in the end unlike Othello whose deadly revenge is death.

He further uses an imagery of a dried-up fountain. His blood is a symbol of being dried up and not producing any offspring because his wife is tainted. He tops it up with a vulgar imagery of frogs copulating instead of him.

"Or keep it as a cistern for foul toads
To knot and gender"

Othello comments on her beauty,

"Who art so lovely fair."

We can feel his inner conflicts and his pain – his love for his wife and his desire for revenge. His wife is still confused,

"what ignorant sin have I committed?"

Notice that earlier in the play Othello spoke in verse but now he speaks in prose because his status took a nose-dive.

He calls his wife a 'whore' and a 'strumpet' – exceedingly derogatory terms.

In his fury his speech is also sprinkled with vivid imagery. He uses personification to give vent to his wrath,

"Heaven stops the nose at it, and the moon winks"

Heaven stops breathing and the moon closes its eyes because they are too disgusted at Desdemona's promiscuous behaviour. She is mortified at his accusations,

"By heaven you do me wrong!"

TEXT ACT 4 scene 2

OTHELLO
What, not a whore?
DESDEMONA
No, as I shall be saved.
OTHELLO
Is 't possible?
DESDEMONA
O, heaven forgive us!
OTHELLO
I cry you mercy, then.
I took you for that cunning whore of Venice
That married with Othello.—You, mistress,
***Enter* EMILIA**
That have the office opposite to Saint Peter
And keeps the gate of hell—you, you, ay, you!
We have done our course.
There's money for your pains.
HE *gives her money*
I pray you turn the key and keep our counsel.
HE *exits*

EMILIA
Alas, what does this gentleman conceive?
How do you, madam? How do you, my good lady?
DESDEMONA
Faith, half asleep.
EMILIA
Good madam, what's the matter with my lord?
DESDEMONA
With who?
EMILIA
Why, with my lord, madam.
DESDEMONA
Who is thy lord?
EMILIA
He that is yours, sweet lady.
DESDEMONA
I have none. Do not talk to me, Emilia.
I cannot weep, nor answers have I none
But what should go by water. Prithee, tonight
Lay on my bed my wedding sheets. Remember.
And call thy husband hither.
EMILIA
Here's a change indeed.
SHE *exits*

DESDEMONA
'Tis meet I should be used so, very meet.
How have I been behaved that he might stick
The small'st opinion on my least misuse?

EXPLANATION

He even accuses Emilia of being an accomplice to Desdemona's infidelity. 'Keeps the gate of hell' meaning she keeps watch whilst Desdemona is with Cassio.

Emilia is shocked at Othello's behaviour. We can detect this by her constant questioning. Desdemona is furious and she denounces her husband saying,

"I have none"

It's ironical that she asks Emilia to,

"Lay on my bed my wedding sheets."

Her wedding sheets were symbolic of love and happiness yet now it's become a symbol for death and deceit.

Shakespeare uses dramatic irony because Desdemona asks Emilia to call Iago.

He was the architect of all her woes, now she calls him for assistance, this makes the audience nervous because he will, 'add fuel to the flame with his lies and treachery.

TEXT ACT 4 scene 2

Enter **IAGO** *and* **EMILIA**

IAGO
What is your pleasure, madam? How is 't with you?
DESDEMONA
I cannot tell. Those that do teach young babes
Do it with gentle means and easy tasks.
He might have chid me so, for, in good faith,
I am a child to chiding.
IAGO
What is the matter, lady?
EMILIA
Alas, Iago, my lord hath so bewhored her,
Thrown such despite and heavy terms upon her
As true hearts cannot bear.
DESDEMONA
Am I that name, Iago?
IAGO
What name, fair lady?
DESDEMONA
Such as she said my lord did say I was.
EMILIA
He called her "whore." A beggar in his drink
Could not have laid such terms upon his callet.
IAGO
Why did he so?
DESDEMONA
I do not know. I am sure I am none such.
IAGO
Do not weep, do not weep! Alas the day!
EMILIA
Hath she forsook so many noble matches,
Her father and her country and her friends,
To be called "whore"?
Would it not make one weep?
DESDEMONA
It is my wretched fortune.
IAGO
Beshrew him for 't! How comes this trick upon him?
DESDEMONA
Nay, heaven doth know.
EMILIA
I will be hanged if some eternal villain,
Some busy and insinuating rogue,
Some cogging, cozening slave, to get some office,
Have not devised this slander. I will be hanged else.
IAGO
Fie, there is no such man. It is impossible.

EXPLANATION

Iago is full of pretence when he meets Desdemona and asks her,

"What is the matter, lady."

She tells him that people who teach little children do so gently and kindly. If Othello wanted to reprimand her or teach her, he could have done it in a more dignified manner.

Iago is centre stage once more.
Emilia relays to him the shocking abuse that Othello heaped upon poor Desdemona.
He repeatedly called her a 'whore.'

There's a lot of foreshadowing and dramatic irony in this conversation between Iago and Desdemona.

Iago's pretence galls the audience.

"Why did he so?"

Emilia's response needs to be noted because there's a hint of racism in her tone. She hints that Desdemona had a chance of marrying better, she had better give up,

"Her father and her country and her friends"

She could have married a nobleman, instead of marrying an abusive Black man."

We sincerely sympathise with Desdemona's naivety and innocence because she is pouring her heart out to Iago whose main ambition is to destroy her.

Iago innocently asks,

"How comes this trick upon him?"

Where did he get this horrible idea from?
Here's a classic case of dramatic irony when Emilia unconsciously 'hits the nail on the head' when she slams the evil villain for creating such a slander,

"cogging, cozening slave, to get some office"

DESDEMONA
If any such there be, heaven pardon him.
EMILIA
A halter pardon him, and hell gnaw his bones!
Why should he call her "whore"?
Who keeps her company?
What place? What time? What form?
What likelihood?
The Moor's abused by some most villainous knave,
Some base notorious knave, some scurvy fellow.
O heaven, that such companions thou 'dst unfold,
And put in every honest hand a whip
To lash the rascals naked through the world,
Even from the east to th' west!
IAGO
Speak within door.
EMILIA
O, fie upon them! Some such squire he was
That turned your wit the seamy side without
And made you to suspect me with the Moor.
IAGO
You are a fool. Go to!

DESDEMONA
Alas, Iago,
What shall I do to win my lord again?
Good friend, go to him. For by this light of heaven,
I know not how I lost him.
SHE ***kneels***
Here I kneel.
If e'er my will did trespass 'gainst his love,
Either in discourse of thought or actual deed,
Or that mine eyes, mine ears, or any sense
Delighted them in any other form,
Or that I do not yet, and ever did,
And ever will—though he do shake me off
To beggarly divorcement—love him dearly,
Comfort forswear me!
SHE ***stands.***
Unkindness may do much,
And his unkindness may defeat my life,
But never taint my love. I cannot say "whore"—
It does abhor me now I speak the word.
To do the act that might the addition earn,
Not the world's mass of vanity could make me.

The alliteration revealing her rage. Little does she realise that her husband is responsible for Desdemona's misery and ultimately her death.

Emilia will be horrified to learn that she too was an unwitting accomplice in Desdemona's tragic fate.

Iago's hypocritical and cold responses shocks the audience, the man has an audacity to remark,

"If any such there be, heaven pardon him."

And Emilia gives a perfect response, condemning him to hell,

"and hell gnaw his bones!"

Shakespeare uses dramatic irony because we are well, aware that Iago orchestrated this misery on Desdemona.

She asks him to liaise on her behalf, with her husband not realising that she just 'stepped into the lion's jaws'.

She played right into the hands of Iago.

"Good friend, go to him."

Desdemona wants to apologise if she did Othello any wrong. She pledges her undying love for him. She uses sensory imagery,

"Or that mine eyes, mine ears, or any sense
Delighted them in any other form"

Although he ignores her, 'beggarly divorcement.'

She still loves him dearly.

"never taint my love"

She has never been or never will be the

"whore"

that he claims her to be.

IAGO
I pray you be content. 'Tis but his humour.
The business of the state does him offense,
And he does chide with you.

DESDEMONA
If 'twere no other—

IAGO
It is but so, I warrant.

Trumpets sound

Hark how these instruments summon to supper.
The messengers of Venice stays the meat.
Go in and weep not. All things shall be well.

DESDEMONA *and* EMILIA *exit*

***Enter* RODERIGO**

How now, Roderigo?

RODERIGO
I do not find
That thou deal'st justly with me.

IAGO
What in the contrary?

RODERIGO
Every day thou daff'st me with some device, Iago, and rather, as it seems to me now, keep'st from me all conveniency than suppliest me with the least advantage of hope. I will indeed no longer endure it. Nor am I yet persuaded to put in peace what already I have foolishly suffered.

IAGO
Will you hear me, Roderigo?

RODERIGO
Faith, I have heard too much, and your words
And performances are no kin together.

IAGO
You charge me most unjustly.

RODERIGO
With naught but truth. I have wasted myself out of my means. The jewels you have had from me to deliver to Desdemona would half have corrupted a votaress. You have told me she hath received them, and returned me expectations and comforts of sudden respect and acquaintance, but I find none.

IAGO
Well, go to! Very well.

RODERIGO
"Very well." "Go to!" I cannot go to, man, nor 'tis not very well! By this hand, I say 'tis very scurvy, and begin to find myself fopped in it.

Iago pacifies her with lies insisting that it's the pressure of state business that is causing his bad behaviour.

At least the audience can breathe a sigh of relief.

Roderigo has finally come to his senses albeit a little too late.

He has now acknowledged Iago as a thief and philanderer.

He is forthright in his accusations of Iago's thuggery.

He stole his money and jewellery with the promise of favours from Desdemona which never materialised.

There's a change in tone here – a more light-hearted one as compared to the vulgarisms and brutality of what we have just witnessed.

Roderigo is appalled at Iago's nonchalant, don't care attitude to the devastation he caused.

"Well go to! Very well."

He threatens to expose Iago for his devious behaviour.

Nothing phases Iago, he very lightly dismisses Roderigo and is planning his next move. We hope Roderigo will remain firm in his threats to Iago's lies.

Iago is very smug because he got Roderigo 'twisted around his little finger'.

He threatens to expose his deceit to Desdemona and to ask for his jewellery back. He will also apologise for his silly behaviour. If he doesn't get it back, then he warns that he will deal with Iago very severely. Can he win this challenge?

IAGO
Very well.

RODERIGO
I tell you 'tis not very well! I will make myself known
to Desdemona. If she will return me my jewels,
I will give over my suit and repent my unlawful
solicitation. If not, assure yourself
I will seek satisfaction of you.

IAGO
You have said now.

RODERIGO
Ay, and said nothing
But what I protest intendment of doing.

IAGO
Why, now I see there's mettle in thee, and even
from this instant do build on thee a better opinion
than ever before. Give me thy hand, Roderigo.
Thou hast taken against me a most just exception,
but yet I protest I have dealt
most directly in thy affair.

RODERIGO
It hath not appeared.

IAGO
I grant indeed it hath not appeared, and your
suspicion is not without wit and judgment. But,
Roderigo, if thou hast that in thee indeed which
have greater reason to believe now than ever—
I mean purpose, courage, and valour—this night
show it. If thou the next night following enjoy not
Desdemona, take me from this world with treachery
and devise engines for my life.

RODERIGO
Well, what is it? Is it within reason and compass?

IAGO
Sir, there is especial commission come from
Venice to depute Cassio in Othello's place.

RODERIGO
Is that true?
Why, then, Othello and Desdemona,
Return again to Venice.

IAGO
O, no. He goes into Mauritania and takes away
with him the fair Desdemona, unless his abode be
lingered here by some accident—wherein none
can be so determinate as the removing of Cassio.

RODERIGO
How do you mean, removing him?

IAGO
Why, by making him uncapable of Othello's place:
knocking out his brains.

RODERIGO
And that you would have me to do?

Iago 'sugar-coats' his explanation to Roderigo claiming that he did everything in his power to help him. He also praises Roderigo's boldness,

"Why, now I see there's mettle in thee."

Iago flatters Roderigo and he is instantly sucked in. His gullibility shocks the audience who finds Roderigo's stupidity a form of comic entertainment.

Iago promises that Roderigo will enjoy Desdemona's company if he only waits, otherwise he can kill him.

His lies are so compelling that Roderigo is eager to follow his sick plan of murder.

"Well, what is it? Is it within reason and compass?"

Thus far we know of Iago to be a manipulative, scheming liar but now we can actually witness his brutality like Othello.

He uses an explicit onomatopoeia,

"knocking out his brains."

To further highlight his ruthless, cold and calculated personality.

IAGO

Ay, if you dare do yourself a profit and a right. He sups tonight with a harlotry, and thither will I go to him. He knows not yet of his honourable fortune. If you will watch his going thence (which I will fashion to fall out between twelve and one), you may take him at your pleasure. I will be near to second your attempt, and he shall fall between us. Come, stand not amazed at it, but go along with me. I will show you such a necessity in his death that you Shall think yourself bound to put it on him. It is now high supper time, and the night grows to waste. About it!

RODERIGO

I will hear further reason for this.

IAGO

And you shall be satisfied.

THEY ***exit***

He coaxes Roderigo to waylay and kill Cassio.

He gives detailed plans of Cassio's where abouts.

He says that he will give Roderigo all the reasons why killing Cassio will be beneficial to him.

The audience is puzzled as to how men become 'putty' in Iago's hands.

He mesmerises them with his 'silver tongue' and they believe his dirty lies.

Roderigo is a classic fool who does not win the sympathy of the audience.

TEXT ACT 4 scene 3

Another Room in the Citadel

Enter
OTHELLO, LODOVICO, DESDEMONA,
EMILIA, ***and Attendants***

LODOVICO
I do beseech you, sir, trouble yourself no further.
OTHELLO
O, pardon me, 'twill do me good to walk.
LODOVICO
Madam, good night. I humbly thank your Ladyship.
DESDEMONA
Your Honour is most welcome.
OTHELLO
Will you walk, sir?—O, Desdemona—
DESDEMONA
My lord?
OTHELLO
Get you to bed on th' instant.
I will be returned forthwith.
Dismiss your attendant there.
Look 't be done.
DESDEMONA
I will, my lord.

All but **DESDEMONA** ***and*** **EMILIA** ***exit***

EMILIA
How goes it now? He looks gentler than he did.
DESDEMONA
He says he will return incontinent,
And hath commanded me to go to bed,
And bade me to dismiss you.
EMILIA
Dismiss me?
DESDEMONA
It was his bidding. Therefore, good Emilia,
Give me my nightly wearing, and adieu.
We must not now displease him.
EMILIA
I would you had never seen him.

DESDEMONA
So would not I. My love doth so approve him
That even his stubbornness, his checks, his frowns—
Prithee, unpin me—have grace and favour in them.
EMILIA
I have laid those sheets you bade me on the bed.

EXPLANATION

This scene has ominous undertones and a dramatic sense of foreboding.

Shakespeare softens the blow for the audience and prepares them for the horror of Act 5 by allowing Desdemona to give us a chilling preview into her death.

She foreshadows it by making reference to her death through the mention of various inanimate objects. Othello orders her to go to bed immediately,

"Get you to bed on th' instant"

His dominating attitude towards her is chilling and her subservient, docile attitude to him is endearing.

"I will my lord."

At this point the audience becomes nervous for Desdemona.

When Desdemona tells Emilia that Othello commanded her to dismiss her.

"Dismiss your attendant there"

Emilia responds rather shockingly,

"Dismiss me?"

There's a ring of fear in her tone as though she senses that something is going to go awry.

Once again, we see Emilia's bitterness towards Othello and her distaste for Desdemona's poor choice of a husband

"I would you had never seen him."

She is so clouded by love that she simply cannot sense the danger surrounding her.

"My love doth so approve him
That even his stubbornness
—have grace and favour in them."

She also foreshadows her death and seems to have an uncanny premonition about it.

TEXT ACT 4 scene 3

DESDEMONA
All's one. Good faith, how foolish are our minds!
If I do die before thee, prithee, shroud me
In one of those same sheets.
EMILIA
Come, come, you talk!
DESDEMONA
My mother had a maid called Barbary.
She was in love, and he she loved proved mad
And did forsake her. She had a song of willow,
An old thing 'twas, but it expressed her fortune,
And she died singing it. That song tonight
Will not go from my mind. I have much to do
But to go hang my head all at one side
And sing it like poor Barbary. Prithee, dispatch.
EMILIA
Shall I go fetch your nightgown?
DESDEMONA
No, unpin me here.
This Lodovico is a proper man.
EMILIA
A very handsome man.
DESDEMONA
He speaks well.
EMILIA
I know a lady in Venice would have walked
barefoot to Palestine for a touch of his nether lip.
DESDEMONA, *singing*
The poor soul sat sighing by a sycamore tree,
Sing all a green willow.
Her hand on her bosom, her head on her knee,
Sing willow, willow, willow.
The fresh streams ran by her and murmured
her moans,
Sing willow, willow, willow;
Her salt tears fell from her, and softened
The stones—
Lay by these.
Sing willow, willow, willow.
Prithee hie thee! He'll come anon.
Sing all a green willow must be my garland.
Let nobody blame him, his scorn I approve.
Nay, that's not next. Hark, who is 't that knocks?
EMILIA
It's the wind.

EXPLANATION

Furthermore, Desdemona asks for her nightgown and bed sheets which, one can connote, can symbolise death because death is sometimes referred to as, 'sleeping peacefully,' and the sheets can be symbolic of a shroud.

"If I do die before thee, prithee shroud me
In one of those same sheets"

We can draw a juxtaposition between Emilia's outspoken, forthright attitude to that of Desdemona's love-sick, delusional attitude which frustrates the audience.

Shakespeare employs some very unique writing styles to tug at the audience's heartstrings (a sad but poignant love song) sung by Desdemona herself.

Barbary's love song is a reflection of her current situation of woe with her crazed husband.

Desdemona too just like Barbary has to hang her head to one side and sing this lamentable song. This song is constantly ringing in Desdemona's mind.

"That song tonight
Will not go from my mind."

There is a certain eerie, deep sense of foreboding in the air as though Desdemona is preparing for her death. Barbary died singing this same song. Will Desdemona follow suit?

The tension is so palpable you can, 'cut it with a knife.' Shakespeare cuts the tension by adding Desdemona's comments about Lodovico,

"This Lodovico is a proper man."

DESDEMONA
I called my love false love,
but what said he then?
Sing willow, willow, willow.
If I court more women, you'll couch with
more men.
So, get thee gone. Good night. Mine eyes do itch;
Doth that bode weeping?

EMILIA
'Tis neither here nor there.

DESDEMONA
I have heard it said so. O these men, these men!
Dost thou in conscience think—tell me, Emilia—
That there be women do abuse their husbands
In such gross kind?

EMILIA
There be some such, no question.

DESDEMONA
Wouldst thou do such a deed for all the world?

EMILIA
Why, would not you?

DESDEMONA
No, by this heavenly light!

EMILIA
Nor I neither, by this heavenly light.
I might do 't as well i' th' dark.

DESDEMONA
Wouldst thou do such a deed for all the world?

EMILIA
The world's a huge thing.
It is a great price for a small vice.

The fact that she is admiring another man apart from her husband tends to lessen our deep sympathy for her, hence helping us to accept her death a little more easily later on.

She complains that her eyes itch and senses that it is an ominous sign that she will be crying soon.

"Mine eyes do itch;
Doth that bode weeping?"

We can detect Desdemona's pain in this soulful exclamation,

"O these men, these men!"

Her sheer innocence and naivety are so appealing because she didn't know that wives commit adultery and she can't fathom out why,

"That There be women do abuse their husbands?"

yet she became the innocent victim of the very idea of adultery – something she totally abhors.

Sadly, she uses biblical imagery to proclaim her innocence, to no avail.

"No, by this heavenly light!"

When asked if she would commit adultery Emilia makes a joke of it saying she would rather do it in the dark.

Note that both women mention 'heavenly light'. One can connote that Desdemona will soon be seeing the 'heavenly light'.

Desdemona is aghast and shocked at Emilia's revelation.

"Wouldst thou do such a deed for all the world?"

DESDEMONA
In troth, I think thou wouldst not.

EMILIA
In troth, I think I should, and undo 't when I had
done it. Marry, I would not do such a thing for a
joint ring, nor for measures of lawn, nor for gowns,
petticoats, nor caps, nor any petty exhibition.
But for the whole world—'Uds pity!
Who would not make her husband a cuckold
to make him a monarch?
I should venture purgatory for 't.

DESDEMONA
Beshrew me if I would do such a wrong
For the whole world!

EMILIA
Why, the wrong is but a wrong i' th' world;
and, having the world for your labour,
'tis a wrong in your own world,
and you might quickly make it Right.

DESDEMONA
I do not think there is any such woman.

EMILIA
Yes, a dozen; and as many to th' vantage as
would store the world they played for.
But I do think it is their husbands' faults
If wives do fall. Say that they slack their duties,
And pour our treasures into foreign laps.
Or else break out in peevish jealousies,
Throwing restraint upon us.
Or say they strike us,
Or scant our former having in despite.
Why, we have galls,
and though we have some grace,
Yet have we some revenge. Let husbands know
Their wives have sense like them.
They see, and smell,
And have their palates both for sweet and sour,
As husbands have. What is it that they do
When they change us for others? Is it sport?
I think it is. And doth affection breed it?
I think it doth. Is 't frailty that thus errs?
It is so too. And have not we affections,
Desires for sport, and frailty, as men have?
Then let them use us well. Else let them know,
The ills we do, their ills instruct us so.

DESDEMONA
Good night, good night. God me such uses send,
Not to pick bad from bad, but by bad mend!

Exeunt

Despite Emilia's elaborate explanation about her reasons for committing adultery,

"Who would not make her husband a cuckold to make him a monarch?"

Desdemona stands firm in her belief that women should not cheat on their husbands, and she still cannot believe that such a type of woman exists,

"I do not think there is any such woman."

Emilia insists that there are cheating wives', but she makes an excuse for them saying that it is the husband's fault because they neglect their wives, 'slack their duties' and they, have love affairs with other women,

"And pour our treasures into foreign laps."

Emilia is very streetwise and knowledge- able about the psychology of men. If we look at the relationship between her and Iago, it's obvious that she is harbouring a lot of pent- up frustrations and rage about how Iago treats her.

Emilia's outbursts, by the use of repeated questions,

"When they change us for others? Is it sport?"

reveals her down-trodden status as a woman, as we saw earlier when Iago belittled her and says that she talks too much and when she insists that the culprit will pay for causing Desdemona's sadness. In Act 4 scene 2 line 170, Iago tells Emilia,

"You are a fool. Go to."

Desdemona hopes that this lesson will teach her to learn from this and refute any bad actions.

ACT 5

SUMMARY

In scene 1

- In a dark street in Cyprus Iago directs Roderigo how to kill Cassio but he is wounded by Cassio instead.
- Iago is concerned that Roderigo will ask for his money and his jewellery and he will expose his fraud, so this fight will serve a dual purpose, both Cassio and Roderigo will have to die.
- In the scuffle, Iago steps in and stabs Cassio in the leg. Othello hears his screams and thinks that he is dead.
- Lodovico and Gratiano comes out when it is safe and help the wounded Cassio.
- Iago stabs Roderigo and he dies from his wounds after calling Iago a 'dog'
- Bianca is bewildered at seeing Cassio stabbed and she is mercilessly insulted by Iago who blames her for Cassio's injury.
- Emilia is furious and she too pours scorn on Bianca who promptly denies the accusations.
- Roderigo's body is located, and Iago tells Emilia to notify Othello and Desdemona of these incidents.

In scene 2

- Desdemona is asleep and Othello decides to kill her so that she does not trap more men.
- He kisses her and Desdemona awakens and is bewildered when Othello tells her that he is going to kill her.
- She must pay for her betrayal. She begs him to spare her life or even wait for her to pray, but he strangles her.
- Emilia comes with news of Roderigo's death while trying to kill Cassio.
- To Othello's horror Desdemona suddenly stirs and proclaims that she was responsible for her own death and then dies.
- Emilia is inconsolable and she rants and raves at Othello and threatens to expose him.
- She is also disgusted at her husband's involvement in the deaths and gives a full and emotive account of the handkerchief and Iago's treachery is revealed.
- Iago stabs Emilia who remained loyal to Desdemona to the very end. She lays beside Desdemona and dies.
- Othello is horrified at this revelation and how he was tricked by this fiend Iago.
- He is ashamed of his actions and he confesses to the murder.
- Iago's atrocities are fully exposed, and the guards bring him in. Iago remains silent and does not reveal his intentions.
- Othello kills himself and Lodovico is so incensed at Iago's unspeakable acts of crime that he enlists Cassio, who is the new governor to torture Iago in any way he see – a punishment that will befit his crimes.

TEXT ACT 5 scene 1

At Night in a Street

Enter
IAGO *and* RODERIGO

IAGO
Here, stand behind this bulk. Straight will he come.
Wear thy good rapier bare, and put it home.
Quick, quick! Fear nothing. I'll be at thy elbow.
It makes us or it mars us—think on that,
And fix most firm thy resolution.
RODERIGO
Be near at hand. I may miscarry in 't.
IAGO
Here, at thy hand. Be bold and take thy stand.
HE *moves aside*

RODERIGO
I have no great devotion to the deed,
And yet he hath given me satisfying reasons.
'Tis but a man gone. Forth, my sword! He dies.
HE *draws his sword*

IAGO*, aside*
I have rubbed this young quat almost to the sense,
And he grows angry. Now, whether he kill Cassio,
Or Cassio him, or each do kill the other,
Every way makes my gain. Live Roderigo,
He calls me to a restitution large
Of gold and jewels that I bobbed from him
As gifts to Desdemona.
It must not be. If Cassio do remain,
He hath a daily beauty in his life
That makes me ugly. And besides, the Moor
May unfold me to him. There stand I in much peril.
No, he must die. Be 't so. I hear him coming.

***Enter* CASSIO**
RODERIGO
I know his gait. 'Tis he!—Villain, thou diest!
HE *thrusts at* CASSIO

CASSIO
That thrust had been mine enemy indeed
But that my coat is better than thou know'st.
I will make proof of thine.
HE *draws, and stabs* RODERIGO

EXPLANATION

The pace of this scene moves very fast and Iago's and Roderigo's clandestine intentions are carried out in the cover of darkness. It's 'make or break' for Iago because this plan has to be successful, otherwise he will be in grave danger, of his wretchedness being exposed.

Othello will kill him as promised. He managed to manipulate Roderigo right to the very end and now he even got him to resort to murder.

He is still the master leader directing Roderigo how to kill Cassio,

"Quick, quick! Fear nothing. I'll be at thy elbow."

Roderigo says that Cassio gave him reasons to kill him. He shockingly says that it's only one man,

" 'Tis but a man gone."

as though taking his life doesn't matter.

Iago calls Roderigo a 'worthless' person, 'quat' who is angry. Iago is still triumphant making sure his plans materialise.

Both Cassio and Roderigo must be eliminated so that his vile and devious actions won't be exposed. If Roderigo lives, he will claim all his stolen jewellery and money and if Cassio lives, his lies to Othello will be exposed and Othello will surely kill him.

"No, he must die. Be 't so. I hear him coming

This scene mirrors Act 1 scene 1 where Iago is manipulating Roderigo but now this manipulation has reached its heights culminating in the death of Roderigo

RODERIGO
O, I am slain!

RODERIGO ***falls***
IAGO ***stabs*** **CASSIO** ***in the leg, and exits***

CASSIO
I am maimed forever! Help, ho! Murder, murder!

Enter **OTHELLO**

OTHELLO
The voice of Cassio! Iago keeps his word.
RODERIGO
O, villain that I am!
OTHELLO, *aside*
It is even so.
CASSIO
O, help ho! Light! A surgeon!
OTHELLO, *aside*
'Tis he! O brave Iago, honest and just,
That hast such noble sense of thy friend's wrong!
Thou teachest me.—Minion, your dear lies dead,
And your unblest fate hies. Strumpet, I come.
Forth of my heart those charms,
Thine eyes, are blotted.
Thy bed, lust-stained,
Shall with lust's blood be spotted.

OTHELLO ***exits***
Enter **LODOVICO** ***and*** **GRATIANO**

CASSIO
What ho! No watch? No passage? Murder, murder!
GRATIANO
'Tis some mischance. The voice is very direful.
CASSIO
O, help!
LODOVICO
Hark!
RODERIGO
O wretched villain!
LODOVICO
Two or three groan. 'Tis heavy night.
These may be counterfeits. Let's think 't unsafe
To come in to the cry without more help.
RODERIGO
Nobody come? Then shall I bleed to death.

Roderigo strikes out at Cassio, but Cassio is wearing armour so he in retaliation he stabs Roderigo. Roderigo yells in pain whilst Iago stabs Cassio in the leg. This violent scene moves the action along fast.

Iago's expert skills in his betrayals, deceits, his manipulation and his 'wheeling and dealings' keeps the audience riveted. He seems to be invincible.

The audience is kept in suspense as to whether the long arm of the law will deal him the severe punishment that he deserves.

Othello still calls Iago,

"O brave Iago, honest and just."

Othello's vulgar outburst to Desdemona is frightening. He is now like a crazed man possessed by the devil.

"Thy bed, lust-stained,
Shall with lust's blood be spotted."

Cassio is in agony and screaming for help, Lodovico is scared to venture forth when he heard the screams of pain.

"Two or three groan. 'Tis heavy night.
These may be counterfeits."

Roderigo's plea for help is in vain and he is afraid that he will 'bleed to death'.

Of course, Iago enters with his pyjamas and a light feigning innocence.

Enter* IAGO *with a light

LODOVICO
Hark!
GRATIANO
Here's one comes in his shirt,
With light and weapons.
IAGO
Who's there?
Whose noise is this that cries on murder?
LODOVICO
We do not know.
IAGO
Did not you hear a cry?
CASSIO
Here, here! For heaven's sake, help me!
IAGO
What's the matter?
GRATIANO, *to Lodovico*
This is Othello's ancient, as I take it.
LODOVICO
The same indeed, a very valiant fellow.
IAGO, *to Cassio*
What are you here that cry so grievously?
CASSIO
Iago? O, I am spoiled, undone by villains.
Give me some help!
IAGO
O me, lieutenant! What villains have done this?
CASSIO
I think that one of them is hereabout
And cannot make away.
IAGO
O treacherous villains!
to Lodovico and Gratiano.
What are you there?
Come in, and give some help.
RODERIGO
O, help me here!
CASSIO
That's one of them.
IAGO, *to Roderigo*
O murd'rous slave! O villain!
HE *stabs Roderigo*

RODERIGO
O damned Iago! O inhuman dog!
IAGO
Kill men i' th' dark?—
Where be these bloody thieves?
How silent is this town! Ho, murder, murder!—
What may you be? Are you of good or evil?

Iago is carrying a light and weapons. These juxtaposed objects is symbolic because one can connote that Iago needs the light in his life to get rid of the darkness that he is so deeply steeped in.

The weapons can be symbolic of all the pain and suffering he has caused. He was the living weapon that cause untold pain and suffering and even innocent people to die.

Iago is pretending to be helpful. Cassio pleads to him for help and still trusts him,

"Iago? O, I am spoiled, undone by villains."

Ironically, unbeknown to him the villain is Iago himself. But Iago shrewdly replies,

"What villains have done this?"

Iago is 'ruling the roost' right to the very end, giving commands, belting out instructions, hence causing a twist in the plot when he stabs Roderigo blaming him for Cassio's wound which he deliberately caused.

"O murd'rous slave! O villain!"

Only on his deathbed was Roderigo able to see how Iago destroyed him- his willing, innocent victim.

"O damned Iago! O inhuman dog!"

He uses apt animal imagery to describe Iago's animalistic character albeit too late.

TEXT ACT 5 scene 1

LODOVICO
As you shall prove us, praise us.
IAGO
Signior Lodovico?
LODOVICO
He, sir.
IAGO
I cry you mercy. Here's Cassio hurt by villains.
GRATIANO
Cassio?
IAGO
How is 't, brother?
CASSIO
My leg is cut in two.
IAGO
Marry, heaven forbid!
Light, gentlemen. I'll bind it with my shirt.

***Enter* BIANCA**

BIANCA
What is the matter, ho? Who is 't that cried?
IAGO
Who is 't that cried?
BIANCA
O, my dear Cassio,
My sweet Cassio! O Cassio, Cassio, Cassio!
IAGO
O notable strumpet! Cassio, may you suspect
Who they should be that have thus mangled you?
CASSIO
No.
GRATIANO
I am sorry to find you thus; I have been to seek you.
IAGO
Lend me a garter. So.—O for a chair
To bear him easily hence!
BIANCA
Alas, he faints. O, Cassio, Cassio, Cassio!
IAGO
Gentlemen all, I do suspect this trash
To be a party in this injury.—
Patience awhile, good Cassio.—Come, come;
Lend me a light.
Peering at Roderigo
Know we this face or no?
Alas, my friend and my dear countryman
Roderigo? No! Yes, sure. O heaven, Roderigo!
GRATIANO
What, of Venice?

EXPLANATION

When Lodovico arrives, Iago pretends to be all caring and tells them that Cassio is 'hurt by villains'.

The hypocrisy of it all, Iago has the audaciousness of calling him 'brother' after causing him a grievous harm and then agrees to bind Cassio's wound with his shirt. How frustratingly altruistic Iago pretends to be.

Bianca is genuinely distraught when she sees injured Cassio.

Iago's belittling of Bianca is shocking, he calls her a 'whore' and very conveniently chose to use her as a 'scapegoat',

His quick witted, devious mind blamed Bianca for Cassio's injury,

"I do suspect this trash
To be a party in this injury.—"

When we look at all the women of the Elizabethan and Renaissance periods, it's obvious that women were treated with disdain and occupied a very inferior position in society.

All the women in the play are treated in a derogatory manner. Here innocent Bianca becomes Iago's victim.

Iago takes his viciousness further when he cunningly calls Roderigo,

"my friend and my dear countryman"

after killing him.

IAGO
Even he, sir. Did you know him?
GRATIANO
Know him? Ay.
IAGO
Signior Gratiano? I cry your gentle pardon.
These bloody accidents must excuse my manners
That so neglected you.
GRATIANO
I am glad to see you.
IAGO
How do you, Cassio?—O, a chair, a chair!
GRATIANO
Roderigo?
IAGO
He, he, 'tis he!
A chair is brought in
O, that's well said; the chair.—
Some good man bear him carefully from hence.
I'll fetch the General's surgeon.—
to Bianca
For you, mistress,
Save you your labour.
He that lies slain here, Cassio
Was my dear friend. What malice was between you?
CASSIO
None in the world. Nor do I know the man.
IAGO, *to Bianca*
What, look you pale?—O, bear him out o' th' air.

CASSIO, *in the chair, and* RODERIGO *are carried off*

to Gratiano and Lodovico.
Stay you, good gentlemen.—
Look you pale, mistress?—
Do you perceive the gastness of her eye?—
Nay, if you stare, we shall hear more anon.—
Behold her well. I pray you, look upon her.
Do you see, gentlemen? Nay, guiltiness will speak
Though tongues were out of use.

Shakespeare gives us a flurry of activity in Iago, he's apologising to Gratiano,

"I cry your gentle pardon."

Then

"O, a chair, a chair!"

He then directs that Cassio be taken out,

"bear him carefully from hence"

Then his attention is focused on Bianca,

"For you mistress,
Save your labour"

Then his focus is turned to Cassio,

"What malice was between you?"

He is doing many things at the same time. This can suggest Iago's nervousness hence he's increasing the pace and pushing the action of the play forward very quickly.

Iago is forced to do this to cover up his malicious deeds. He has to think and act very quickly so that his conniving plot is not exposed. If it is, then he is in serious trouble.

The plot thickens - Iago hurls abuse at innocent Bianca, accusing her of a plot to hurt Cassio by using constant questioning to make her feel guilty,

"Look you pale, mistress?"

"Do you see gentleman?"

***Enter* EMILIA**

EMILIA
Alas, what is the matter?
What is the matter, husband?
IAGO
Cassio hath here been set on in the dark
By Roderigo and fellows that are scaped.
He's almost slain, and Roderigo dead.
EMILIA
Alas, good gentleman! Alas, good Cassio!
IAGO
This is the fruits of whoring. Prithee, Emilia,
Go know of Cassio where he supped tonight.
To Bianca
What, do you shake at that?
BIANCA
He supped at my house, but I therefore shake not.
IAGO
O, did he so? I charge you go with me.
EMILIA
O fie upon thee, strumpet!
BIANCA
I am no strumpet, but of life as honest
As you that thus abuse me.
EMILIA
As I? Faugh! Fie upon to
IAGO
Kind gentlemen, let's go see poor Cassio dressed.—
Come, mistress, you must tell 's another tale.—
Emilia, run you to the citadel
And tell my lord and lady what hath happed.—
Will you go on afore? *Aside.* This is the night
That either makes me or fordoes me quite.

They exit in different directions

The constant use of the hyphens also suggests that Iago is waiting for the men's approval to find Bianca guilty.

Emilia enters, all exasperated and demands to know what happened. Iago is unfazed and coolly tells her what had happened.

In his icy cold tone, he blames Cassio's 'whoring' for his injury,

"fruits of his whoring"

He still insists that Bianca is guilty,

"What, do you shake at that?"

He orders Bianca to go with him. Iago is so convincing that Emilia believes him, and she turns on Bianca with a bitter tone and verbally attacks her.

"O fie upon thee, strumpet!"

Bianca tries to defend herself but is outwitted by Emilia.

"I am no strumpet"

Iago very ominously remarks,

"This is the night
That either makes me or fordoes me quite."

We will see!

TEXT ACT 5 scene 2

A Chamber in the Citadel

Enter
OTHELLO ***with a light***
DESDEMONA ***in her bed***

OTHELLO
It is the cause, it is the cause, my soul.
Let me not name it to you, you chaste stars.
It is the cause. Yet I'll not shed her blood,
Nor scar that whiter skin of hers than snow,
And smooth as monumental alabaster.
Yet she must die, else she'll betray more men.
Put out the light, and then put out the light.
If I quench thee, thou flaming minister,
I can again thy former light restore
Should I repent me. But once put out thy light,
Thou cunning'st pattern of excelling nature,
I know not where is that Promethean heat
That can thy light relume.
When I have plucked the rose,
I cannot give it vital growth again.
It needs must wither. I'll smell it on the tree.
O balmy breath, that dost almost persuade
Justice to break her sword!

He kisses her

One more, one more.
Be thus when thou art dead, and I will kill thee
And love thee after. One more, and this the last.

He kisses her

So sweet was ne'er so fatal. I must weep,
But they are cruel tears. This sorrow's heavenly:
It strikes where it doth love. She wakes.

DESDEMONA
Who's there? Othello?

OTHELLO
Ay, Desdemona.

DESDEMONA
Will you come to bed, my lord?

OTHELLO
Have you prayed tonight, Desdemona?

DESDEMONA
Ay, my lord.

OTHELLO
If you bethink yourself of any crime
Unreconciled as yet to heaven and grace,
Solicit for it straight.

DESDEMONA
Alack, my lord,
What may you mean by that?

EXPLANATION

This scene is full of pathos and disillusion-ment. It's very emotional and it gets the audience emotionally involved. It's the climax that they have been waiting for – to see how Iago's well-laid plans materialise.

This scene moves at a slow, sluggish pace.

Othello's soliloquy is threatening and unnerving and the tension and suspense is riveting. The repetition,

"It is the cause, it is the cause, my soul."

suggests his sheer determination to kill his wife. He speaks to the heavenly body,

"you chaste stars"

Ironically, he's going to destroy his wife's chastity because of his jealousy. He refused to scar,

"that whiter skin of hers than snow"

His use of the superlative, 'whiter' and the simile, 'than snow' suggests Desdemona's innocence and purity.

He uses a simile,

"And smooth as monumental alabaster"

is an ominous foreshadowing of death because alabaster is associated with tombs and are used to create monuments of angels and sculptures for the dead.

He tries to justify his action because he believes that if she lives, she will betray more men,

"Yet she must die, else she'll betray more men."

He uses light imagery,

"Put out the light,"

It's symbolic of Othello extinguishing his wife's light by killing her.

TEXT ACT 5 scene 2

OTHELLO
Well, do it, and be brief. I will walk by.
I would not kill thy unpreparèd spirit.
No, heaven forfend! I would not kill thy soul.

DESDEMONA
Talk you of killing?

OTHELLO
Ay, I do.

DESDEMONA
Then heaven have mercy on me.

OTHELLO
Amen, with all my heart.

DESDEMONA
If you say so, I hope you will not kill me.

OTHELLO
Humh.

DESDEMONA
And yet I fear you, for you're fatal then
When your eyes roll so.
Why I should fear I know not
Since guiltiness I know not, but yet I feel I fear.

OTHELLO
Think on thy sins.

DESDEMONA
They are loves I bear to you.

OTHELLO
Ay, and for that thou diest.

DESDEMONA
That death's unnatural that kills for loving.
Alas, why gnaw you so your nether lip?
Some bloody passion shakes your very frame.
These are portents, but yet I hope, I hope
They do not point on me.

OTHELLO
Peace, and be still.

DESDEMONA
I will so. What's the matter?

OTHELLO
That handkerchief
Which I so loved, and gave thee,
Thou gav'st to Cassio.

EXPLANATION

He says that once he kills her, he can never restore her back to life again.

He compares her to a rose, once plucked it cannot grow again.

He mercilessly asks her if she had prayed, and he demands that she atone for her sins.

He wants her soul to be prepared for heaven. Desdemona is confused at her husband's strange requests.

"No, heaven forfend! I would not kill thy soul"

Shakespeare uses dramatic irony here because the audience knows Desdemona's fate and there's nail-biting suspense about Othello's intentions.

Desdemona expresses her fear, and she is terrified,

"for you're fatal then
When your eyes roll so."

She is not guilty but she's still afraid of him.
She is like a trapped animal and Othello asks her to,

"Think on thy sins."

She confesses her love for him, and he tells her she has to die for that. She notices his altered physical appearance because he is biting his lip and shaking,

"Some bloody passion shakes your very frame."

It is his jealous passion that will lead to a deadly end.

She has a premonition and ominously believes that his appearance are bad omens, and she hopes that it will not affect her life.

He broaches the subject of the handkerchief to her and insists that she gave it to Cassio.

TEXT ACT 5 scene 2

DESDEMONA
No, by my life and soul! Send for the man
And ask him.
OTHELLO
Sweet soul, take heed, take heed of perjury.
Thou art on thy deathbed.
DESDEMONA
Ay, but not yet to die.
OTHELLO
Yes, presently.
Therefore confess thee freely of thy sin.
For to deny each article with oath
Cannot remove nor choke the strong conception
That I do groan withal. Thou art to die.
DESDEMONA
Then Lord have mercy on me!
OTHELLO
I say "Amen."
DESDEMONA
And have you mercy, too. I never did
Offend you in my life, never loved Cassio
But with such general warranty of heaven
As I might love. I never gave him token.
OTHELLO
By heaven, I saw my handkerchief in 's hand!
O perjured woman, thou dost stone my heart
And mak'st me call what I intend to do
A murder, which I thought a sacrifice!
I saw the handkerchief!
DESDEMONA
He found it, then.
I never gave it him. Send for him hither.
Let him confess a truth.
OTHELLO
He hath confessed.
DESDEMONA
What, my lord?
OTHELLO
That he hath used thee.
DESDEMONA
How? Unlawfully?
OTHELLO
Ay.
DESDEMONA
He will not say so.
OTHELLO
No. His mouth is stopped.
Honest Iago hath ta'en order for 't.
DESDEMONA
O, my fear interprets. What, is he dead?

EXPLANATION

Desdemona vehemently denied it,

"No, by my life and soul! Send for the man
And ask him."

He insists that she confesses her sin and even if she denies everything, he will still not believe her.

She will die anyway so he leaves her no option. She begs for his mercy,

"And have you mercy, too. I never did
Offend you in my life"

It's ironical that both Desdemona and Othello make use of religious imagery, 'heaven' sadly it's where Desdemona will soon be heading.

He says that she had turned his heart into stone.

"thou dost stone my heart."

And she gave him thoughts to murder. She challenges him and asks for Cassio to come and tell him the truth.

"Let him confess a truth."

Othello rejects this

"He hath confessed"

And lied that Cassio said that he had a physical relationship with her.

We have to draw a juxtaposition between Othello's character in act one to his behaviour now. There's a steep downward slide from celebrated, well-respected war hero to a tragic hero. Even his language has changed from standard to non-standard English- riddled with vulgar colloquialism.

He is caught up in a web of lies and he has taken leave of his senses. He lies to Desdemona that Cassio admitted having a physical relationship with her and 'Honest' Iago had killed him.

TEXT ACT 5 scene 2

OTHELLO
Had all his hairs been lives, my great revenge
Had stomach for them all.
DESDEMONA
Alas, he is betrayed, and I undone.
SHE ***weeps***
OTHELLO
Out, strumpet! Weep'st thou for him to my face?
DESDEMONA
O banish me, my lord, but kill me not!
OTHELLO
Down, strumpet!
DESDEMONA
Kill me tomorrow, let me live tonight.
OTHELLO
Nay, if you strive—
DESDEMONA
But half an hour!
OTHELLO
Being done, there is no pause.
DESDEMONA
But while I say one prayer!
OTHELLO
It is too late.

OTHELLO *smothers* DESDEMONA

EMILIA, *within*
My lord, my lord? What ho! My lord, my lord!
OTHELLO
What noise is this?—Not dead? Not yet quite dead?
I that am cruel am yet merciful.
I would not have thee linger in thy pain.
So, so.
EMILIA, *within*
What, ho! My lord, my lord!
OTHELLO
Who's there?
EMILIA, *within*
O, good my lord, I would speak a word with you.
OTHELLO
Yes. 'Tis Emilia.—By and by.—She's dead.
'Tis like she comes to speak of Cassio's death.
The noise was here. Ha, no more moving?
Still as the grave. Shall she come in? Were 't good?
I think she stirs again. No. What's best to do?
If she come in, she'll sure speak to my wife.
My wife, my wife! What wife? I have no wife.
O insupportable! O heavy hour!
Methinks it should be now a huge eclipse
Of sun and moon, and that th' affrighted globe
Should yawn at alteration.

EXPLANATION

Othello becomes furious when his wife shows concern,

"Alas, he is betrayed, and I undone."

He thinks that she is weeping for her lover, and he verbally abuses her calling her a whore,

"Out, strumpet! Weep'st thou for him to my face?"

Desdemona's pleas to stay alive is gut-wrenching,

"O banish me my lord but kill me not."

"Kill me tomorrow, let me live tonight."

But ruthless, cold-hearted Othello smothers her despite her asking to say one prayer,

"But while I say one prayer!"

The exclamation can suggest a finality – her death. He says that he is,

"cruel - yet merciful"

He don't want her to suffer, because she didn't die immediately 'linger in thy pain,' he planned to kill her quickly and with no blood.
Emilia arrives and Othello is unnerved.

The simile,

"Still as the grave."

Is rather symbolic because Desdemona is dead and is still like the grave, where she is heading.

Othello repeats the phrase, 'My wife' several times, using exclamation and questions suggesting his untold pain and agitation.

"O insupportable! O heavy hour!"

He wishes for an eclipse because Desdemona is absent from the earth. In his pain and agony, he lets Emilia in.

EMILIA, *within*
I do beseech you
That I may speak with you. O, good my lord—
OTHELLO
I had forgot thee. O, come in, Emilia.—
Soft, by and by, let me the curtains draw.—
Where art thou?

Enter **EMILIA**

What's the matter with thee now?
EMILIA
O, my good lord, yonder's foul murders done.
OTHELLO
What? Now?
EMILIA
But now, my lord.
OTHELLO
It is the very error of the moon.
She comes more nearer Earth than she was wont
And makes men mad.
EMILIA
Cassio, my lord, hath killed
A young Venetian called Roderigo.
OTHELLO
Roderigo killed? And Cassio killed?
EMILIA
No, Cassio is not killed.
OTHELLO
Not Cassio killed? Then murder's out of tune,
And sweet revenge grows harsh.
DESDEMONA
O falsely, falsely murdered.
EMILIA
O Lord, what cry is that?
OTHELLO
That? What?
EMILIA
Out, and alas, that was my lady's voice!
Help! Help ho! Help! O lady, speak again!
Sweet Desdemona, O sweet mistress, speak!
DESDEMONA
A guiltless death I die.
EMILIA
O, who hath done this deed?
DESDEMONA
Nobody. I myself. Farewell.
Commend me to my kind lord. O, farewell.

DESDEMONA *dies*

Outspoken Emilia is the voice of reasoning here. She comes in at strategic points in the play and she gives some intelligent input to calm the raging waters. Very expressively she relays to Othello the news about the 'murders'.

Othello very conveniently blames man's crazy behaviour on the moon, saying it comes too close to earth and makes man mad.

He further personifies the 'moon' giving it female qualities, addressing the 'moon' as 'She.' One can connote that he is referring to Desdemona, who drove him crazy and made him kill her.

When Othello learns that Cassio is still alive, he is shocked

"Not Cassio killed? Then murder's out of tune."

But Desdemona suddenly cries out,

"O falsely, falsely murdered."

Othello and Emilia are startled. Emilia cries out desperately,

"Help! Help ho! Help! O lady, speak again!"

The repeated exclamations marks suggest the desperation and pain in Desdemona's voice. Desdemona says that she died an innocent death,

"A guiltless death I die."

And she was responsible for it.

"Nobody. I myself. Farewell.
Commend me to my kind lord. O, farewell."

Desdemona was loyal and respectful to Othello even in death. The poignancy here is that this quality – her lack of hate and revenge, endears her more to the audience, who find her death too painful.

TEXT ACT 5 scene 2

OTHELLO
Why, how should she be murdered?
EMILIA
Alas, who knows?
OTHELLO
You heard her say herself, it was not I.
EMILIA
She said so. I must needs report the truth.
OTHELLO
She's like a liar gone to burning hell!
'Twas I that killed her.
EMILIA
O, the more angel she, and you the blacker devil!
OTHELLO
She turned to folly, and she was a whore.
EMILIA
Thou dost belie her, and thou art a devil!
OTHELLO
She was false as water.
EMILIA
Thou art rash as fire to say
That she was false. O, she was heavenly true!
OTHELLO
Cassio did top her. Ask thy husband else.
O, I were damned beneath all depth in hell
But that I did proceed upon just grounds
To this extremity. Thy husband knew it all.
EMILIA
My husband?
OTHELLO
Thy husband.
EMILIA
That she was false to wedlock?
OTHELLO
Ay, with Cassio. Had she been true,
If heaven would make me such another world
Of one entire and perfect chrysolite,
I'd not have sold her for it.
EMILIA
My husband?
OTHELLO
Ay, 'twas he that told me on her first.
An honest man he is, and hates the slime
That sticks on filthy deeds.
EMILIA
My husband?
OTHELLO
What needs this iterance, woman?
I say, thy husband.
EMILIA
O mistress, villainy hath made mocks with love!—
My husband say she was false?

EXPLANATION

Othello denies killing her, but his rage got the better of him and he then ranted,

"She's like a liar gone to burning hell!
'Twas I that killed her."

Emilia is stupefied, her racist prejudices come to the fore, once again, she uses the superlative 'blacker' attacking his colour and associating him to the devil,

"O the more angel she, and you the blacker devil!"

She tells him firmly that Desdemona was,

"heavenly true!"

Othello reveals that Iago told him that Cassio had a relationship with Desdemona.

Emilia is in utter shock at this revelation. One can depict this by her constant utterances of

"My husband?"

Even Othello questions her about repeating the phrase,

"thy husband"

He said that even God wouldn't have allowed him to sell Desdemona for the world. Sadly, Othello still believes that Iago is,

"An honest man he is, and hates the slime"

Emilia is aghast and she cries out in pain to Desdemona,

"O mistress, villainy hath made mocks with love!"

She is furious and she curses Iago saying that his soul will rot in hell, that he is lying through his teeth and that she was faithful to that 'filthy' marriage.

OTHELLO
He, woman.
I say thy husband. Dost understand the word?
My friend, thy husband; honest, honest Iago.

EMILIA
If he say so, may his pernicious soul
Rot half a grain a day! He lies to th' heart!
She was too fond of her most filthy bargain.

OTHELLO ***draws his sword***

OTHELLO
Hah?

EMILIA
Do thy worst!
This deed of thine is no more worthy heaven
Than thou wast worthy her.

OTHELLO
Peace, you were best!

EMILIA
Thou hast not half that power to do me harm
As I have to be hurt. O gull! O dolt,
As ignorant as dirt! Thou hast done a deed—
I care not for thy sword. I'll make thee known,
Though I lost twenty lives. Help! Help, ho! Help!
The Moor hath killed my mistress!
Murder, murder!

Enter
MONTANO, ***GRATIANO, and*** **IAGO**

MONTANO
What is the matter? How now, general?

EMILIA
O, are you come, Iago? You have done well,
That men must lay their murders on your neck.

GRATIANO
What is the matter?

EMILIA*, to Iago*
Disprove this villain, if thou be'st a man.
He says thou told'st him that his wife was false.
I know thou didst not. Thou 'rt not such a villain.
Speak, for my heart is full.

IAGO
I told him what I thought, and told no more
Than what he found himself was apt and true.

EMILIA
But did you ever tell him she was false?

IAGO
I did.

Emilia is bold and not afraid to speak her mind.

Note that women of the Elizabethan and Jacobean eras were not allowed to voice their concerns.

The penalty for that is swift and deadly, as we see Othello draws his sword for her, despite her female status.

She challenges him and says that he was not 'worthy' of Desdemona. He commands her to be quiet. She rants obscenities at him,

"O gull! O dolt,
As ignorant as dirt!"

and she threatens to expose his vile deed.

"The Moor hath killed my mistress!"

Notice she calls him by name just like Iago did when Othello had a fit. This shows their lack of respect for the fallen hero.

Emilia attacks Iago, yelling that he is responsible for the murders,

"That men must lay their murders on your neck."

She stands her ground and insists that Iago tell the truth because he is not a villain.

Iago tries to wiggle his way out of yet another sticky situation, saying that he only relayed what he thought and no more.

"I told him what I thought, and told no more
Than what he found himself was apt and true"

We admire Emilia because she is so passionate about Desdemona and she's defending her honour to the hilt.

EMILIA
You told a lie, an odious, damnèd lie!
Upon my soul, a lie, a wicked lie!
She false with Cassio? Did you say with Cassio?
IAGO
With Cassio, mistress. Go to! Charm your tongue.
EMILIA
I will not charm my tongue. I am bound to speak.
My mistress here lies murdered in her bed.
ALL
O heavens forfend!
EMILIA, *to Iago*
And your reports have set the murder on!
OTHELLO
Nay, stare not, masters; it is true indeed.
GRATIANO
'Tis a strange truth.
MONTANO
O monstrous act!
EMILIA
Villainy, villainy, villainy!
I think upon 't, I think! I smell 't! O villainy!
I thought so then. I'll kill myself for grief!
O villainy! Villainy!
IAGO
What, are you mad? I charge you get you home.
EMILIA
Good gentlemen, let me have leave to speak.
'Tis proper I obey him, but not now.
Perchance, Iago, I will ne'er go home.
OTHELLO
Oh, Oh, Oh!

OTHELLO ***falls on the bed***

EMILIA
Nay, lay thee down, and roar!
For thou hast killed the sweetest innocent
That e'er did lift up eye.
OTHELLO, *standing*
O, she was foul!—
I scarce did know you, uncle. There lies your niece,
Whose breath indeed
These hands have newly stopped.
I know this act shows horrible and grim.
GRATIANO
Poor Desdemona, I am glad thy father's dead.
Thy match was mortal to him, and pure grief
Shore his old thread in twain. Did he live now,
This sight would make him do a desperate turn,
Yea, curse his better angel from his side,
And fall to reprobance.
My father gave my mother.

She is ranting and raving with lots of exclamations, questions and a stream of expletives to express her outrage.

"You told a lie, an odious, damnèd lie!
Upon my soul, a lie, a wicked lie!"

Iago tries to shut her up, but she won't have it,

"I will not charm my tongue. I am bound to speak."

There's a reversal of the normal order here where in a male-dominated society, the men are at the mercy of a woman's lashing tongue. Does this bode well for Emilia?

"Villainy, villainy, villainy!
I think upon 't, I think! I smell 't! O villainy!
I thought so then. I'll kill myself for grief!
O villainy! Villainy!"

We are overwhelmed at Emilia's loyalty. She rants and raves about her mistress's death.

" I'll kill myself for grief."

She unwittingly foreshadows her own death.

"Perchance, Iago, I will ne'er go home."

Will she ever?
Desdemona's uncle is very distraught,

"Poor Desdemona, I am glad thy father's dead."

Her marriage to the Moor broke his heart in two and that it was 'pure grief' which sent him to an early grave.

Had he lived to see such a dreadful sight – his beautiful daughter lying dead, he would have taken dreadful steps.

Othello insists that Iago knows that she had a physical relationship with Cassio a 'thousand' times.

OTHELLO
'Tis pitiful. But yet Iago knows
That she with Cassio hath the act of shame
A thousand times committed. Cassio confessed it,
And she did gratify his amorous works
With that recognizance and pledge of love
Which I first gave her. I saw it in his hand.
It was a handkerchief, an antique token

EMILIA
O God! O heavenly God!

IAGO
Zounds, hold your peace!

EMILIA
'Twill out, 'twill out. I peace?
No, I will speak as liberal as the north.
Let heaven and men and devils, let them all,
All, all, cry shame against me, yet I'll speak.

IAGO
Be wise, and get you home.

IAGO ***draws his sword***

EMILIA
I will not.

GRATIANO
Fie, your sword upon a woman!

EMILIA
O thou dull Moor, that handkerchief thou speak'st of
I found by fortune, and did give my husband—
For often, with a solemn earnestness
More than indeed belonged to such a trifle,
He begged of me to steal 't.

IAGO
Villainous whore!

EMILIA
She give it Cassio? No, alas, I found it,
And I did give 't my husband.

IAGO
Filth, thou liest!

EMILIA
By heaven, I do not, I do not, gentlemen!
To Othello
O murd'rous coxcomb, what should such a fool
Do with so good a wife?

He even confessed to this rendezvous. He saw the handkerchief, which was a token of his love for Desdemona in Cassio's hand. She gave it to Cassio for 'his amorous works'.

At hearing this Emilia is horrified she yells out,

"O God! O heavenly God!"

Emilia is raging mad and Iago deadly scared.

The audience is aware of Iago's viciousness, and they are becoming nervous for Emilia and hopes she'll hold her tongue for her own safety.

She is overwhelmed with passion and exposes Iago's vile lies.

"No I will speak as liberal as the north."

He warns her (a threat never to be ignored)

"Be wise, and get you home."

She vehemently declares, "I will not." Hence sealing her fate.

Iago draws his sword and Gratiano is shocked that he will draw his sword for a woman.

"Fie, your sword upon a woman!"

She relates the story of the handkerchief and how Iago begged her to steal it. Iago is livid and slanders her,

"villainous whore!"

He denies it and insists that she is lying.

Now he has become a desperate trapped animal because the truth is slowly being revealed.

She yells at Othello for being such a fool to have listened to Iago's lies and kill such a good wife.

TEXT ACT 5 scene 2

OTHELLO
Are there no stones in heaven
But what serves for the thunder?—Precious villain!

The* MOOR *runs at* IAGO *but is disarmed
IAGO *kills his wife*

GRATIANO
The woman falls! Sure he hath killed his wife.
EMILIA
Ay, ay! O, lay me by my mistress' side.

IAGO *exit*

GRATIANO
He's gone, but his wife's killed.

MONTANO
'Tis a notorious villain. Take you this weapon
Which I have here recovered from the Moor.
Come, guard the door without. Let him not pass,
But kill him rather. I'll after that same villain,
For 'tis a damnèd slave.

MONTANO *and* GRATIANO *exit*

OTHELLO
I am not valiant neither,
But every puny whipster gets my sword.
But why should honor outlive honesty?
Let it go all.
EMILIA
What did thy song bode, lady?
Hark, canst thou hear me? I will play the swan
And die in music.
She sings. *Willow, willow, willow.*
Moor, she was chaste. She loved thee, cruel Moor.
So come my soul to bliss, as I speak true.
So speaking as I think, alas, I die.

EMILIA *dies*

OTHELLO
I have another weapon in this chamber.
It is a sword of Spain, the ice brook's temper.
O, here it is.—Uncle, I must come forth.
GRATIANO, *within*
If thou attempt it, it will cost thee dear;
Thou hast no weapon and perforce must suffer.
OTHELLO
Look in upon me, then, and speak with me,
Or naked as I am I will assault thee

EXPLANATION

Finally, Othello learns about Iago's lies and he is furious.

"Precious villain!"

Othello is a broken man, and he runs after Iago, but he is disarmed, but sadly Iago seized the opportunity to kill his wife.

Even to death Emilia was a loyal and faithful servant to Desdemona.

Her sacrifice can have a religious connotation and can be compared to that of Jesus who died on the cross to save the world and she died saving her mistress's honour and dignity.

Finally, Iago and his wickedness has been exposed and he is trying to escape. Montana goes after him,

"I'll after that same villain,
For 'tis a damnèd slave."

Othello has now lost all strength and honour. He has to let it go.

This fallen, tragic hero has lost it all. The flaw in his character – his passionate jealousy made him fall from ranks of accolades as a great soldier to that of murderous villain.

Ironically, Emilia sings the same song that Desdemona sang before she died and both women declared Desdemona's innocence.

Note how these two women mirror each other in virtue and how Othello and Iago mirrored each other in vice.

There's a certain lull in this scene, a certain acceptance of fate. Othello and Iago are victims of their own deadly actions and must suffer the consequences. Othello is desperate and threatens to attack Gratiano.

"Or naked as I am I will assault thee"

Compare Othello now, — he is a crazed prisoner — to that of Act 1.

Enter **GRATIANO**

GRATIANO
What is the matter?

OTHELLO
Behold, I have a weapon.
A better never did itself sustain
Upon a soldier's thigh. I have seen the day
That with this little arm and this good sword
I have made my way through more impediments
Than twenty times your stop. But—O vain boast!
Who can control his fate? 'Tis not so now.
Be not afraid, though you do see me weaponed.
Here is my journey's end, here is my butt
And very sea-mark of my utmost sail.
Do you go back dismayed? 'Tis a lost fear.
Man but a rush against Othello's breast,
And he retires. Where should Othello go?

OTHELLO ***looks toward the bed***

Now, how dost thou look now? O ill-starred wench,
Pale as thy smock, when we shall meet at compt,
This look of thine will hurl my soul from heaven,
And fiends will snatch at it. Cold, cold, my girl?
Even like thy chastity.—O cursed, cursed slave!—
Whip me, you devils,
From the possession of this heavenly sight!
Blow me about in winds, roast me in sulfur,
Wash me in steep-down gulfs of liquid fire!
O, Desdemona! Desdemona! Dead! Oh! Oh!

Enter
LODOVICO, CASSIO ***in a chair,***
MONTANO, ***and*** **IAGO,** ***with Officers***

LODOVICO
Where is this rash and most unfortunate man?

OTHELLO
That's he that was Othello. Here I am.

LODOVICO
Where is that viper? Bring the villain forth.

IAGO ***is brought forward***

OTHELLO
I look down towards his feet; but that's a fable.—
If that thou be'st a devil, I cannot kill thee.

OTHELLO ***stabs*** **IAGO**

LODOVICO
Wrench his sword from him.

You can't help but be astonished at a man who had it all and then chose to lose it because he just couldn't control his passions.

Now he has a sharp, deadly sword that he used to win the war.

"But – O vain boast!"

He says it's no use boasting now and asks who can control his fate. He has accepted his fate and he is calm. He understands that he has come to the end of his journey.

"Here is my journeys end"

This speech reeks of regret. He paints a very sad picture for us. He wants the ultimate punishment for his guilt. He uses biblical imagery,

"This look of thine will hurl my soul from heaven"

He is damned. He asks the devils to 'whip' him for his crime and 'roast' him 'in sulfur'.

"Whip me" — "roast me in sulfur"

His cry to Desdemona is full of remorse and pain,

"O Desdemona! Desdemona! Dead! Oh!"

Lodovico enquires after Othello and Othello answers,

"That's he that was Othello."

Here I am. Othello speaks of himself in the past tense saying that he is no more the perfect gentleman he used to be.

Lodovico aptly calls Iago a 'viper' and 'villain' But Othello calls him the devil and stabs him.

OTHELLO ***is disarmed***

IAGO
I bleed, sir, but not killed.
OTHELLO
I am not sorry neither. I'd have thee live,
For in my sense 'tis happiness to die.
LODOVICO
O thou Othello, that wert once so good,
Fall'n in the practice of a damned slave,
What shall be said to thee?
OTHELLO
Why, anything.
An honourable murderer, if you will,
For naught I did in hate, but all in honour.
LODOVICO
This wretch hath part confessed his villainy.
Did you and he consent in Cassio's death?
OTHELLO
Ay.
CASSIO
Dear general, I never gave you cause.
OTHELLO
I do believe it, and I ask your pardon.
Will you, I pray, demand that demi-devil
Why he hath thus ensnared my soul and body?
IAGO
Demand me nothing. What you know, you know.
From this time forth I never will speak word.
LODOVICO
What? Not to pray?
GRATIANO
Torments will ope your lips.
OTHELLO
Well, thou dost best.
LODOVICO
Sir, You shall understand what hath befall'n,
Which, as I think, you know not. Here is a letter
Found in the pocket of the slain Roderigo,
And here another.
HE ***shows papers***
The one of them imports
The death of Cassio, to be undertook
By Roderigo.
OTHELLO
O villain!
CASSIO
Most heathenish and most gross.
LODOVICO
Now here's another discontented paper
Found in his pocket, too; and this it seems
Roderigo meant t' have sent this damned villain,
But that, belike, Iago in the interim
Came in and satisfied him.

Right to the very end Iago taunts people and exposes his vile side;

"I bleed, sir, but not killed."

This is a very moving, emotive conclusion to the play. Our tragic hero has completely fallen, after confessing his crimes, yet Lodovico still pity him and so does the audience.

He was enticed by Iago the 'damned slave'. Sadly though, Othello tries to cling onto some shreds of his honour and asked to be called,

"An honourable murderer"

He tries to justify his actions by saying that he didn't kill Desdemona out of hate but because of his honour.

A woman's chastity, in the Jacobean era was a man's honour and if he is a cuckold he is regarded as an object of derision.

Othello needs answers from Iago for wrecking his life and torturing him,

"Why he hath thus ensnared my soul and body?"

Iago's arrogance and lack of remorse is staggering. He prefers to stay silent, but all his crimes are exposed through letters found in Roderigo's pockets.

Othello is astounded when he learns of Iago's devious ploys, 'O villain!' and Cassio says,

"Most heathenish and most gross."

Othello finally gets the truth about the handkerchief. He asks Cassio how it came to be in his possession, and he tells Othello that he found it in his chambers and Iago confessed to deliberately dropping it there to cause mischief.

OTHELLO
O, thou pernicious caitiff!—
How came you, Cassio, by that handkerchief
That was my wife's?
CASSIO
I found it in my chamber.
And he himself confessed it but even now,
That there he dropped it for a special purpose
Which wrought to his desire.
OTHELLO
O fool, fool, fool!
CASSIO
There is besides, in Roderigo's letter,
How he upbraids Iago, that he made him
Brave me upon the watch, whereon it came
That I was cast. And even but now he spake,
After long seeming dead: Iago hurt him,
Iago set him on
LODOVICO, *to Othello*
You must forsake this room and go with us.
Your power and your command is taken off,
And Cassio rules in Cyprus. For this slave,
If there be any cunning cruelty
That can torment him much and hold him long,
It shall be his. You shall close prisoner rest,
Till that the nature of your fault be known
To the Venetian state.—Come, bring away.
OTHELLO
Soft you. A word or two before you go.
I have done the state some service, and they know 't
No more of that. I pray you in your letters,
When you shall these unlucky deeds relate,
Speak of me as I am. Nothing extenuate,
Nor set down aught in malice. Then must you speak
Of one that loved not wisely, but too well;
Of one not easily jealous, but being wrought,
Perplexed in the extreme; of one whose hand,
Like the base Judean, threw a pearl away
Richer than all his tribe; of one whose subdued eyes,
Albeit unused to the melting mood,
Drops tears as fast as the Arabian trees
Their medicinable gum. Set you down this.
And say besides, that in Aleppo once,
Where a malignant and a turbanned Turk
Beat a Venetian and traduced the state,
I took by th' throat the circumcised dog,
And smote him, thus.

OTHELLO ***stabs himself***

Othello is overwrought with rage, and we see his regret in this painful utterance,

"O fool, fool, fool!"

Cassio also relays how Iago set Roderigo up to annoy him and cause a fight so that he will get dismissed from his post.

Iago was the sole architect of their untold misery with his unspeakable crimes, but he still remains unscathed and remorseless.

Shakespeare's Othello is a tragedy of mammoth proportions. It had all the ingredients - love, jealousy, greed, hate, to enrich the plot and keep the audience riveted from the beginning to end.

A single character Iago was the driving force behind all the action causing chaos and mayhem in people's lives for no apparent reason, and the audience is satisfied that he got his 'just deserts' in the end.

Iago was the sole architect of their untold misery with his unspeakable crimes, but he still remains unscathed and remorseless.

Shakespeare's Othello is a tragedy of mammoth proportions. It had all the ingredients - love, jealousy, greed, hate, to enrich the plot and keep the audience riveted from the beginning to end.

LODOVICO
O bloody period!
GRATIANO
All that is spoke is marred.
OTHELLO, *to Desdemona*
I kissed thee ere I killed thee. No way but this,
Killing myself, to die upon a kiss.

OTHELLO ***dies.***

CASSIO
This did I fear, but thought he had no weapon,
For he was great of heart.

LODOVICO, *to Iago*
O Spartan dog,
More fell than anguish, hunger, or the sea,
Look on the tragic loading of this bed.
This is thy work.—The object poisons sight.
Let it be hid.—Gratiano, keep the house,
And seize upon the fortunes of the Moor,
For they succeed on you.
to Cassio.
To you, lord governor,
Remains the censure of this hellish villain.
The time, the place, the torture, O, enforce it.
Myself will straight aboard, and to the state
This heavy act with heavy heart relate.

THEY ***exit***

A single character Iago was the driving force behind all the action causing chaos and mayhem in people's lives for no apparent reason, and the audience is satisfied that he got his 'just deserts' in the end.

Lodovico takes control and wrap up things. Cassio will rule in Cyprus and he will be responsible for Iago's torture.

Othello's speech is very sad and poignant before he dies.

He was a brave and dutiful soldier, and he asks to be described as one who loved too passionately but who was not wise enough to see through this 'Base Judean.'

The use of his biblical imagery refers to Judas who betrayed Jesus for thirty pieces of silver. He too was betrayed by Iago for his position. He gives us a sad anecdote about how he killed a Turk and then stabs himself.

Othello speaks to Desdemona and tells her that whilst he is dying, he is kissing her.

"Killing myself, to die upon a kiss."

Cassio praises Othello as a great gentleman,

"For he was great of heart."

Lodovico unleashes a tirade of abuse against Iago calling him,

"O Spartan dog"

and he tells him that all the tragedy lying on the bed was orchestrated by his evil, pathetic acts.

"This is thy work. – The object poisons sight."

Lodovico hopes that Cassio will give Iago, the 'hellish villain' –

"The time, the place, the torture, O, enforce it."

He aught to give to Iago all the untold pain and suffering that he has caused.

OTHELLO

- Othello is a protagonist who was a general in the army for the Venetian state
- Well- respected by the state of Venice because of his military success
- Comes from noble birth but being a Black man his status in Venetian society is controversial
- He turns tragic hero in the end
- He is sent to Cyprus during the conflict with the Turks to act as governor
- He elopes with Desdemona which infuriates Brabantio, her father
- As black man in high society Venice a lot of controversy surrounds him
- Before we meet him, Iago gives us a lot of controversial ideas about Othello being lascivious and immoral
- This clouded view gives us a negative impression of Othello
- When we meet him, he proves to be a well-spoken, sincere, decent, honest gentleman
- He is a figure of authority in the army and commands respect
- He carries out his duties in Cyprus with much dedication – keeping the peace and inspecting the fortifications
- He speaks in blank verse at the beginning but sadly, this changes to prose later in the play
- He was a perfect husband and lover as seen in the sentimental love token – handkerchief given to Desdemona
- Othello and Desdemona shared a deep, mutual love and respect despite colour boundaries
- Iago's greed, jealousy and overpowering urge for revenge destroys this deep bond
- When he meets her in Cyprus his love overflows but later, he looks on her with derision and asks her to leave
- Iago goads Othello into believing that Desdemona was being unfaithful with Cassio and jealousy reigns
- Othello's honour and his wife's chastity, was of paramount importance right to the very end
- Iago presented tangible evidence like the handkerchief to prove that Desdemona was unfaithful.
- Othello entrusts his complete faith in Iago and even acts like him calling him 'honest Iago'
- Iago's lies and deceit catapults Othello towards becoming a tragic hero
- Othello's decision is catastrophic when he kills his innocent wife in a savage way
- He courageously atones for his sin by committing suicide, and the audience pities him
- In the end he became a tragic hero and turns from protagonist to antagonist

DESDEMONA

- The daughter of a wealthy Venetian whose father refers to her as his 'jewel'
- She is the female protagonist and the victim in this tragic play
- She is beautiful, with a depth of passion, good social graces and empathetic
- Her father is convinced that she is innocent, and Othello kidnapped or used witchcraft to subdue her
- But he soon discovers that she was an active participant
- She is very strong-willed and determined and had no qualms about eloping with a Black man
- She defies her father and stands by her husband and gently submits to her husband
- Sadly, in the end, her boldness vanishes when she becomes fearful of Othello
- She is vibrant, young, and energetic and her sexuality is exploited by Iago
- He maliciously uses it against her which ultimately culminates in her death
- Iago accuses her of having an affair with Cassio which enrages Othello, and he is consumed with jealousy
- This sets off a series of dramatic events ending in a deadly plot to kill her
- She goads Othello relentlessly to reinstate Cassio and this can be misconstrued as her having too much of Cassio's interest at heart
- Just before she dies, she hears that Cassio is dead and she shows concern which infuriates Othello
- Her capacity to love is her greatest strength and she upheld it even to death
- Her loyalty to her husband is phenomenal when she defends him on her deathbed absolving him of her death
- Even when he accuses her of infidelity and even physically and emotionally abuse her, she says; "Even his stubbornness, his cheeks and frowns have grace and favour in them."
- She is absolutely shocked when she is accused of infidelity, and she questions Emilia if such women exist
- Her name Desdemona means 'unfortunate' and sadly she became a symbol of misfortune
- She is innocently accused of infidelity, her reputation tarnished and her husband withdrawing his love from her
- She is so naïve and innocent, that she even blames herself for her own death – two major factors that led to her catastrophic death
- She became Iago's unwitting pawn in his deadly game of malice and revenge
- She was not worldly like Emilia and her innocence shines, with her conversation with Emilia about infidelity
- She insists that she will never ever commit adultery but ironically that's the very thing she was wrongly accused of which led to her terrible demise
- Her pleading for her life at the end was gut-wrenching and this stunning but gullible heroine stole the hearts of the audience

IAGO

- The creation of a complex and emotionally detached character like Iago is Shakespeare's masterpiece.
- His ruthless and unfathomable character keeps the audience spellbound, rendering him a compelling Machiavellian character.
- His ruthless intellectualism, his inherent evil and his cold, calculating manipulation staggers the audience.
- He is the classic example of an artistic, brilliant villain in a revenge tragedy.
- He very skilfully manages to utilise the weaknesses of every character to weave a web of lies and deceit without anyone noticing until the very end.
- At the beginning he complains about being ordinary when Cassio got the job, "Preferment goes by letter and affection" but this enigmatic character managed to get everyone including his superiors 'on their knees.'
- This destructive, malignant character is the epitome of the theme of appearance versus reality. He says, "I am not what I am."
- He always appears so courteous and caring, offering plausible advice yet in reality he is the 'devil incarnate.'
- There is a certain mystery surrounding this paranoid villain because his true motives for such degradation of people's morals are unclear, if not petty. Critics have accused him of possessing a 'motiveless malignity.'
- He envied Othello's physical union with Desdemona, and very crudely says that Desdemona is 'sport for Jove' and 'full of game.' And she is in the 'gross clasps of a lascivious Moor.' Iago is seething from sexual and professional jealousy and is 'hell bent' on taking revenge.
- He makes 'no bones' about his misogynistic and racist views associating Othello to, 'an old black ram' and a 'Barbary horse.' Note the use of the animal imagery.
- Desdemona is the 'white ewe' and Othello the 'black ram.'
- Iago controls the action, sets the pace and the mood, manipulates the characters, speaking in both prose and blank verse in particular situations and he assumes centre stage with all the attention on him.
- He is a convincing actor who can play many roles and has the intelligence to manipulate any situation.
- Because of his misogynistic views he treats all women with disdain. He makes bawdy, vulgar insinuations about Desdemona's sexuality and blatantly calls Bianca a 'whore'. He even blames her for causing Cassio's injury.
- His brusque tone with Emilia is unnerving. He only speaks to her cordially when he wants something.
- She has to do his bidding or suffer the consequences – death.
- He tries to create a false bond between Othello and himself by convincing him that he is 'honest' and has his interest at heart.

- He manipulated the very core of a reputable character and reduced him to a murderer.
- He declares his love for Othello and tries to replace Desdemona's affection. He hunted Othello down like a prey and wrought havoc in his life until he sought the ultimate revenge when Othello took his own life.
- He was professionally jealous of Cassio's rise to lieutenant and his charm, so he concocted the plan with Roderigo to get him fired.
- His relationship with Roderigo was motivated by greed, he saw his weakness for love and capitalised on that and robbed him for his money and jewellery, eventually killing him.
- In the end, although Iago still maintained his power by being silent, all his atrocities were exposed, and he got the apt punishment for all his evil deeds – torture.

RODGERIO

- He is a wealthy Venetian gentleman, one of the 'curled darlings of Venetian Society', who is in love with Desdemona.
- He is a very controversial character, and the audience don't know whether to feel sorry for him or be angry with him.
- He adds spice and humour to the plot, hence cutting the tension at times.
- He becomes Iago's victim in his deadly plot and paid the ultimate price eventually.
- It's almost comic to see how he lacks all sense of reasoning and allows Iago to abuse and manipulate him.
- Towards the end he threatens Iago that he is going to leave Cyprus and also expose him, apologise to Desdemona and claim his jewels and money from her.
- Just when the audience breathe a sigh of relief that he's finally manning up, he is goaded by Iago to kill Cassio.
- We are disappointed to see a vile side to him like Iago. He was prepared to kill Cassio saying, it's just one and that he gave him reason to do so.
- Furthermore, he is unable to see that this is unrequited love and refused to accept the fact that Desdemona loves and is married to Othello. This is very selfish of him.
- He was unable to see through Iago's devilish behaviour, although it was glaring at him because he gave him all that money and jewellery but still didn't get to enjoy Desdemona.
- Only in the end when Iago stabs him, he comes to realise the truth and yells out, 'inhuman dog' albeit too late.

EMILIA

- Emilia is Iago's faithful but scorned wife and Desdemona's lady in waiting. There's a bit of controversy surrounding her because she is caught between, 'The Devil and the deep blue sea.'
- She has to adhere to all Iago's demands and cannot be wholly faithful to Desdemona. She gives the handkerchief to Iago who asked her to steal it but she couldn't perceive that he will make mischief with it.
- Even at the end she refused to believe that her husband was involved in these atrocities, and she repeatedly utters the words, 'My husband' several times to the chagrin of Othello.
- She also lies when Desdemona asks for the handkerchief, "I know not Madam."
- But in the end, she made up for this, she fought ferociously, exposing her husband's vile deeds to defend Desdemona's honour.
- She is maltreated and scorned on in public by Iago, especially when she insists that Cassio and Desdemona are not having an affair.
- She is the voice of reasoning and very knowledgeable on the topic of men. She justifies to Desdemona, why women should cheat, and 'make their husbands kings.'
- She was also furious with Othello when she heard that he killed Desdemona and she levelled all kind of verbal abuse at him.
- Despite Iago's shabby treatment of her, she remains loyal to him and she verbally abused Bianca when Iago lied to her that Bianca was responsible for Cassio's attack.
- Nevertheless, in the end she proved to be the strongest woman in the play. She vehemently denies that Desdemona is guilty of infidelity. She exposes all Iago's lies and challenges him to tell the truth. She also detailed the story of the handkerchief which infuriated Iago.
- He tells her that if she knows best, she will go home, but she refused and she wouldn't be silenced.
- She fought with might and power to save Desdemona's honour.
- Her passion shocks the audience, and we are sorry that she so nobly sacrificed her life for the love and loyalty of her mistress.
- "I'll kill myself for grief." These words are poignant and a reflection of her love and kindness. She asked to be laid next to her mistress and she sang the same song that Desdemona sang before she died. A symbol of both women's purity in love.

CASSIO

- He is a soldier from Florence, and he was promoted to lieutenant by Othello.
- They have a good relationship but it later crumbles when Iago lies to Othello that Cassio is having a physical relationship with his wife.
- He is very gallant when he meets Desdemona and heaps praises on her. He also treats Emilia with respect, but Iago's warped mind imagines that Cassio has cuckolded him with Emilia.
- However, we see the ugly side of Cassio when he belittles Bianca although he is having a physical relationship with her.
- Iago also treats him with disdain because he goes with Bianca who is immoral.
- Iago looks for flaws in people and make them his target. He is jealous of Cassio because he believes that he doesn't deserve the post of lieutenant.
- Iago ensured that he concocted a devious plan for Roderigo to annoy Cassio whilst he plied him with alcohol which ensued in a brawl. Othello was furious and he fired Cassio.
- Iago also used him to help materialise his devious plot against Othello.
- He was having a conversation about Bianca, but Othello was made to believe that he was talking about Desdemona.
- Othello saw the handkerchief in his hand and that triggered him off. He was now convinced that Desdemona gave it to him for 'services rendered'.
- In the end he is stabbed by Iago, and he was able to clear up the confusion and Iago's deadly plot began to unravel.
- He was given Othello's position as governor, and he was made responsible by Lodovico to mete out the harshest punishment to evil Iago.

JEALOUSY

- The dominant theme in the play is jealousy. It festers out of a state of depravity, lack of achievement or an innate fear of loss.
- In order to alleviate this overwhelming feeling of jealousy, one must overcome it with malicious acts of hate and revenge as we see the antagonist Iago continues to do, achieving gratification in the end.
- In the play it destroys all form of honour, love and goodness. The characters are powerless to act against this powerful force. They are either the architects of it or it's pitiful victim.
- It has taken a strong hold of the protagonist Othello and he loses total control of his senses and is determined to kill his wife and Cassio who he wrongly believes to be having an affair.
- He uses very strong and violent language, 'tear her all to pieces.' To show his jealous rage. He was devoured by passions of jealousy, the 'green-eyed monster' took complete control of his actions and thoughts.
- Iago says that 'jealousy comes from within." An innate feeling lodged within oneself.
- Iago's is envious of Cassio who got promoted to a post of lieutenant which he desired. He is also jealous of Cassio's mannerisms and status. This however set off a chain of deadly events that moves the plot along and set the play in motion.
- There's a lot of sexual jealousy because Iago is jealous of the sexual union between Desdemona and Othello. He is sarcastic and uses animal imagery to demean it. 'Black ewe tupping your white ewe'
- Iago makes several references to the couple's physical union, furthermore he is so extremely jealous that he believes that Both Cassio and Othello are cuckolding him with Emilia. He is also jealous of Cassio's sexual liaison with Bianca. He verbally abuses her, calling her a 'whore.'
- When Cassio gets hurt, Iago tells Emilia that this is the result for having an affair with a whore.
- Bianca, on the other hand was very jealous when Cassio gave her the handkerchief, thinking it was from another lover.
- Ironically, note that all these characters had no reason to let jealousy cloud their judgement. They paid dearly for their irrational behaviour. Othello kills himself with is sword, Iago will be tortured, Desdemona lost her life and Cassio was injured.

RACISM

- Shakespeare's tragic hero Othello is a Moor from Spain.
- During the Elizabethan and Jacobean periods there seemed to be much racial prejudices against black people.
- There were many negative views associated with them. They were the typical 'villains' or the 'lascivious' type.
- They were also associated to sexual immorality as Iago tries to portray Othello in the play, using animal imagery to describe his sexuality.
- In Medieval paintings the black man was represented by the devil in hell. Hence Othello is referred to 'the devil' on numerous occasions, especially by Emilia and Iago.
- Iago makes several references to Othello's race. He and Brabantio and even Emilia are not thrilled about Desdemona's choice of a husband, and they are very vocal about it.
- Although he was a great soldier of very high ranks and well respected by the Senate of Venice there is still that underlying sense of racism.
- At first, he was portrayed as being loyal, articulate, a good lover and husband and whom the audience admired.
- Sadly though, he plunged into the depths of insanity and ended up killing his wife.
- Although Desdemona loves and respect him – she has no issues with being married to a black man, but Othello feels that she had tired of him and he questions his colour and his age, hinting that he is not good enough for her.
- He doubts his marriage because he believes that this is a reason for her to be unfaithful to him with Cassio.
- Despite being accepted by Venetian Society, Othello still felt like an outsider and was treated like that because of his colour. The characters did not hesitate to use racial slurs against him throughout the play as though it was normal and acceptable.

LOVE, RELATIONSHIPS and FRIENDSHIP

- When discussing the themes of love' it is imperative to look at its context in the Shakespearean era. Men were the dominant pillar in society and women were under the control of the men as seen with the way the women were treated by the men.
- A man's honour was defined by his wife's chastity and any man who was cuckolded regarded it as a slight to his masculinity and honour. Othello said that he did not kill Desdemona out of hate but because of his honour. Different rules applied to both men and women. It was proper for Cassio to indulge with a 'whore' yet Desdemona had to pay with her life for the 'infidelity' that she was wrongfully accused of.
- Another focal point of the play is the theme of love which is explored in several ways. Initially the love between Othello and Desdemona was a perfect mix of harmony and respect but as the play progressed it turned into hate and destruction. Despite their social and cultural differences, they embrace their love openly to everyone.
- The love between Iago and Emilia is one of convenience, where Emilia is used to participate in Iago's deadly plot like provide the handkerchief and to endure his constant tongue- lashing. Iago was jealous of the deep marriage bond between Othello and Desdemona, so he chose to destroy it by besmirching Desdemona's good character by crudely targeting her sexuality.
- Iago's misogynistic character forces him to vilify Emilia, degrade and embarrass Bianca and subject Desdemona to untold cruelty because she had power through her deep love over Othello.
- Iago hated people who were besotted with love. He makes a mockery of Othello and reduces him to a state of insanity making him believe that his love has been replaced. He also thinks that Roderigo is a complete fool for his unrequited love for Desdemona and he uses this to rob him of his money and he makes snide remarks about him several times. His reaction to Cassio's relationship with Bianca is one of mockery because he unreservedly belittles both of them in public.
- The love between Cassio and Bianca is a more one-sided physical affair because Bianca is in love with Cassio, but he just views her as a 'customer' whom he is ashamed of being seen in public with.
- Then there's the unrequited love between Desdemona and Roderigo who actually lost his life just for a delusional fantasy of love. There's also the undying friendship between Emilia, who was prepared to sacrifice her life for her mistress's honour.
- Sadly though, we see that all these women were powerless to act or say anything. They were in the end subjected to unfair treatment and they paid the ultimate penalty. Desdemona was docile and honourable even unto death when she didn't implicate her husband in her death.
- Emilia insisted that she will not be silenced. She put Iago on the spot and tried to illicit the truth from him but was killed.
- Note how both men, Othello and Iago drew out their swords against Emilia and were determined to silence her for trying to infiltrate the man's world of power and dominance.

EXAM STYLE QUESTIONS

[Q1] "The society for which Shakespeare was writing knew only too well that power implies the ability to make victims of individuals."
Discuss the extent to which you consider this to be the case in Othello
Using, as your starting point, Iago's soliloquy
"Thus do I ever make my fool my purse" at the end of Act 1 scene 3.

[Q2] "Despite all the social and personal pressures on him, what ultimately destroys Othello is his own impulse towards self-destruction."
Consider this view of Shakespeare's presentation of Othello through discussion of at least two carefully chosen extracts from the text.

[Q3] **How far do you agree with the claim that "in Othello Shakespeare portrays a society where the greatest power is neither political nor military but lies in the persuasive power of language"?**
You should include in your answer some discussion of the dialogue where Iago keeps advising Roderigo to "put money in your purse".
It is near the end of Act 1 Scene 3.

[Q4] "In his tragedies Shakespeare presents a cynical view of a world where personal relationships are inevitably destructive."
How far do you consider it appropriate to apply this judgement to Othello?
You should include in your answer textual discussion which addresses a minimum of two relationships.

[Q5] "In the world of Shakespeare's play, the greatest suffering is reserved for those who take it upon themselves to become the avengers."
How far do you think this view of Othello is justified?
You should include in your answer some discussion of relevant material from Act 3 Scene 3.

[Q6] "Othello portrays a world that has the same conviction as our own; that stupidity is more destructive than evil."
How far do you find this an acceptable view of Shakespeare's tragedy?
You should include in your answer an examination of at least two relevant extracts from the text.

[Q7] "In Othello Shakespeare explores the nature of social prejudice".
How far does your reading of the play support this view?
You should use as a starting point for your answer a close examination of
Act 1 Scene 2 (from OTHELLO: Holla, stand there") to
Act 1 Scene 3 (down to "BRABANTIO: I have done, my lord")

[Q8] To what extent do you agree that in Othello Shakespeare presents "women as victims of men?"
You should base your answer on a close examination to two or more appropriate sequences of your choice.

[Q9] Remind yourself of Act IV Scene 3 of Othello, the Willow Scene.
Using an examination of this scene as your starting point,
explore Shakespeare's portrayal of Emilia's relationship to her social superiors.
Does she seem to you simply to play the role of a servant or
does Shakespeare also make her integral to the structure of his tragedy?

[Q10]"Shakespeare's presentation of Othello, in his role both as general and as husband, makes it impossible for the modern audience to sympathise with him completely".
How do you react to this view?
You should include in your answer at least two carefully chosen extracts from the text.

[Q11]"To the Shakespearean audience, the notion of mixed marriage was not just unnatural, it was evil and would be punished."
How valid does this comment seem to you when applied to Othello?
You should use as your starting point examination of relevant material
from the central section of Act 1 Scene 3
from the entry of Brabantio, Othello, Cassio, Iago, Roderigo and Officers
to when the Duke says, "Your son-in-law is far more fair than black."

[Q12]"In Shakespeare's day it was central to contemporary assumptions about the nature of tragedy that the tragic hero himself should be noble. That is why this is Othello's tragedy and not, for example, Iago's."
How do you, as a member of a modern Shakespearean audience, react to this comment on Othello?
You should include in your answer an examination of at least two extracts from the text.

[Q13]"In Othello, Shakespeare portrays a morally chaotic world in which love can be even more destructive than hate."
How far do you find this an acceptable view of Shakespeare's tragedy?
In your answer, you should include an examination of relevant material from Act 5 scene 2.

[Q14]It has been argued that in Othello, Shakespeare demonstrates the need of those in power to obey the social and moral conventions of the day; if they do not, the state itself becomes threatened."
What do you think about this interpretation of Shakespeare's tragedy?
In your answer, you should include an examination of at least two carefully chosen extracts from the play.

[Q15]"In the tragedies, Shakespeare portrays a society in which there is one form of morality and justice for men and an entirely different one for women."
How far do you consider this an appropriate criticism when applied to Othello?
You should include in your answer some detailed discussion of appropriate material taken from Act IV, scene 3.

[Q16]"In the tragic world of Shakespeare's plays, Fate is shown as invariably siding with the most malicious."
How far do you consider this a fitting comment on Othello?
Your answer should include some discussion of at least two carefully chosen extracts from the text.

AUTHOR

Evelyn Samuel was born in South Africa, educated at the University of Durban-Westville, gaining a BA in English, Speech and Drama. She then went on to gain a Higher Education Diploma at the University of South Africa, and then onto the UK where her knowledge and skills were applied in educating students to achieve top grades in English Language and Literature up to A-level. Evelyn gained her Qualified Teacher Status in 2006, but in her pursuit to explore new horizons, continued her education gaining Diplomas in teaching English as a Foreign Language' to International Students, 'Writing Stories for Children', and most recently, gaining a Diploma in 'Travel Journalism'. Apart from teaching and writing, Evelyn's interests include travel to exotic places, cycling, dance, cuisine, and exploring new horizons.

www.EveSuperEasyBooks.com
EveSuperEasyBooks@gmail.com

STUDY GUIDE

Evelyn provides an in depth **SUPER SUPER EASY** interpretation of Shakespeare's Othello, a poignant Machiavellian love tragedy, first performed at Whitehall Palace in November 1604. This guide is a must for those students determined to achieve a top grade in English Literature at any level from Key Stage 3 to GCSE to A-level.

STORY LINE

The Ottoman empire is about to invade Cyprus, and the Venetians decide that Othello the Moor is the general to thwart the Turks.

A storm prevents the invasion, but Iago, Othello's Machiavellian ensign, is out to destroy him and Cassio by hatching a plot to convince him that his newly wed wife Desdemona is an adulteress, in love with Cassio.

The plot centres around a handkerchief given by Othello to Desdemona as a love token, which Emilia has found and given to her husband Iago. Iago uses the handkerchief, rumour, and psychology to change Othello from a devoted husband and hero into an enraged husband full of dark thoughts.

Othello is driven by jealousy fuelled by Iago's evil machinations, to murder Desdemona, but when Iago's wife Emilia exposes her husband's evil schemes, later confirmed in a letter by Roderigo, Othello kills himself, and Iago is condemned by law.

www.ingramcontent.com/pod-product-compliance
Lightning Source LLC
Chambersburg PA
CBHW080908190726
48294CB00008B/2012
* 9 7 8 1 7 3 9 9 9 8 1 5 8 *